HOW TO BUILD
WALLS ·
WALKS ·
PATIO FLOORS

A Sunset Book

LANE PUBLISHING CO.   MENLO PARK, CALIFORNIA

Seventh Printing July 1959

First Edition
Copyright 1952

LANE PUBLISHING CO., MENLO PARK, CALIFORNIA
Publishers of *Sunset*, The Magazine of Western Living
PRINTED IN U. S. A.

CONTENTS

ABOUT THIS BOOK . . .

This is one in a series of *Sunset Books* designed to help you to unravel some of the practical problems that confront you when you take your hammer, shovel, and plumb bob in hand and tackle a construction project for your home or garden.

Other *Sunset Books* have told how to build lathhouses, garden work centers, greenhouses, fences, gates, barbecues and outdoor fireplaces. This book, really three-in-one, has staked out the subjects of garden walls, patio paving, and step building.

The three subjects that make up this book share a common denominator. Each calls for a modest understanding of the simple facts of masonry. Walls, pavements, or steps are for the most part assembled from stone or man-made imitations thereof. Before you start building your wall, laying paving, or fitting steps, you will find it handy to know how to mix mortar or concrete; cut bricks, dress stone, saw tile; how to lay up bricks, concrete blocks, adobe bricks, or stone; and how to estimate materials needed for your project. You will also want to know how to build your wall so it won't topple over; to lay paving that won't disappear in the mud or crack when something falls on it; how to build steps that are comfortable to ascend.

With only a few exceptions, the projects described in this book can involve you in a substantial investment of time or money—or both. For this reason, we have described the advantages and disadvantages of each type of material to assist you in making a wise and suitable choice.

In general, most of the materials and projects described can be handled by an amateur who has no more than the usual number of thumbs. A few of the processes do call for a high degree of craftsmanship, know-how, or special and expensive equipment. Although these are best entrusted to a professional, full information is given about them to help you to judge the professional's work or to devise specifications.

Some of the basic craft techniques are the same for two or more construction materials. Such techniques are treated only in one place, in the chapter where you are most likely to need the information, and cross-referred from the other chapters. For your convenience, the major points in each chapter are listed in the analytical table of contents on the preceding page.

Here's to your good right arm!

Osmundson & Staley, Design; Osmundson, Photo

WALLS

WHICH WALL? . . . why?

Some dictionaries have trouble separating walls from fences, considering a wall as a kind of fence and vice versa. For that matter, some city ordinances also refer to the two in the same legal breath.

Anyone who has noticed how walls are being used in modern gardens would dispute such fuzziness. Walls and fences can perform identical functions, it is true, such as marking the line between adjacent properties, but there are many things that a wall can do that a fence cannot.

Low, sturdy walls are used for auxiliary garden furniture, to mark the boundaries between different parts of a garden, and to tie together related elements of a garden plan. A low wall may be used to define the edge of a flower bed. When the annuals behind it are in bloom, it serves unobtrusively as a bench; when they have died down, it becomes the visual boundary of the garden, concealing the empty flower bed behind it, and substituting its own color and texture for the missing blooms.

The sturdiness of wall construction recommends it for jobs that require innate strength, such as retaining soil. The earth may only total a couple of yards in a small raised bed, or it may be a whole sloping hillside.

Walls can be used as a focal point of garden design. More easily than wood, masonry can be paired off with water as part of a reflecting pool or lily pond, or as a background for a sheet of falling water. It can also stand up against fire, as part of a barbecue or an outdoor fireplace.

The high, 6-foot masonry wall can serve more than its traditional purpose of marking the boundary of an imposing estate. In a modest garden, the tall wall can be put to good use. A substantial brick or adobe wall will deaden sound effectively, and is often constructed along a busy thoroughfare to deaden the noise of traffic; or as part of an outdoor room, it provides a measure of privacy to neighbors on both sides of it—you can be sure you are answering your own guest, rather than your neighbor's guest a few feet away.

Related to its sound-deadening qualities, a masonry wall also has insulating capacity. In hot climates, it is often chosen as a protection against the merciless rays of the sun. In cold climates, this factor is sometimes a handicap. Masonry walls may require careful placement to keep them from trapping cold air and creating dank, dungeon-like pockets in the garden.

TALK TO YOUR CITY HALL

A masonry wall gains most of its strength from careful and informed construction practices.

A freestanding garden wall is a heavy structure, even though it supports only its own weight. It must be provided with a solid foundation to prevent its being broken apart by frost action or heaving soil. In severe climates, walls must be bedded below frost level. If a wall is to be built across filled or unstable soil, it may require piers extending to firm soil, steel reinforcement, or other special strengthening devices.

Your City Hall will be interested in your plans for a wall. In most cities, a building permit is required; in many areas, the height, set-back, and structural requirements are detailed in the local building codes. Building inspectors are prone to look upon any sized wall that runs along a sidewalk or alley as a potential hazard to the public, and consequently they require assurances of good workmanship and design. In some cities, the property line starts several feet back from the sidewalk, and it is illegal to build right to the edge of the walk.

You will need to secure permission from the city before building a wall that is now, or will later be, load-bearing or that will serve as a retaining wall. Within some cities, you can build a masonry wall higher than the conventional 6 feet, providing it is set well back from the property line.

CONSTRUCTION

The week-end mason should be able to construct a freestanding masonry wall, particularly a low one, without too much difficulty. When he gets up to the 6-foot mark, he may find it more arduous because of the problem of lifting heavy materials to that height. Nor should he have difficulty with low retaining walls if he follows directions carefully; but if he has a serious soil-retaining problem to work out, he should proceed with caution—and with sound professional advice.

The amateur wall builder has several reliable materials to choose from:

Easiest to assemble are the block walls, built of brick, concrete block, or adobe block. Walls made of the large-sized adobe or concrete blocks are quickly erected, require less mason's time. A single adobe block, for instance, equals five clay bricks. On the other hand, bricks are warm-toned, universally obtainable, less tiring to handle.

An amateur with a feeling for natural materials will enjoy piecing together a wall of stone, for more craftsmanship is exacted by stone than by any of the other materials.

Poured concrete is a flexible and easily placed material—up to a certain point. Above 3 or 4 feet, it calls for experienced hands and plenty of equipment.

Osmundson-Staley, Design; Philip Fein, Photo

Redwood seat wall doubles as retainer for raised bed. Wall capped with 2x8 is 24 inches high, maximum for comfort

SEAT WALLS . . . practical, easy to build

A low wall of seat height, thoughtfully placed in the landscape plan, is an attractive and useful addition to any garden. The sweep of the wall through the yard emphasizes design and helps to relate the elements of a garden.

It is one piece of outdoor furniture that can be used the year around and doesn't have to be carted in and out with the changes in weather. It provides extra seating capacity to accommodate an overflow of guests. It can serve as an extemporaneous table, potting bench, or pot display shelf. It may also double as a curb or retainer around planting beds.

If you do the work yourself, wood construction is simplest and easiest, although even an amateur can handle masonry for a low wall without too much difficulty. For information about building masonry walls, see the chapters on those subjects.

CONSTRUCTION

Rules for constructing a wooden seat wall are simple enough. Principal admonition is to build it sturdier than you think necessary.

Lytton & Whitney, Design; Philip Fein, Photo

Wall with exposed posts and V-groove siding on inside, encloses a decorative bed of beach stones and driftwood

A TYPICAL PEDESTAL DETAIL FOR BENCH...

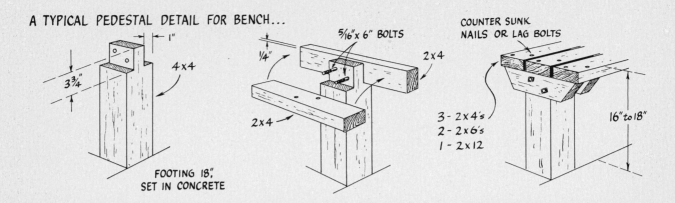

1"

3¾"

4x4

FOOTING 18",
SET IN CONCRETE

5/16" x 6" BOLTS

¼"

2x4

2x4

COUNTER SUNK
NAILS OR LAG BOLTS

3 - 2x4's
2 - 2x6's
1 - 2x12

16" to 18"

ALTERNATE BENCH PEDESTALS...

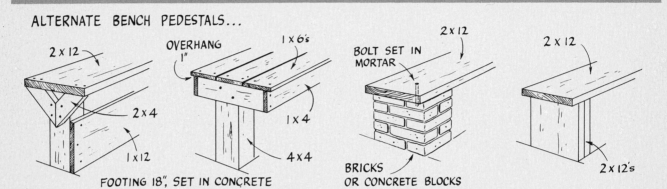

2 x 12

2 x 4

1 x 12

FOOTING 18", SET IN CONCRETE

OVERHANG
1"

1 x 6's

1 x 4

4 x 4

2 x 12

BOLT SET IN
MORTAR

BRICKS
OR CONCRETE BLOCKS

2 x 12

2 x 12's

MITRED CORNER...

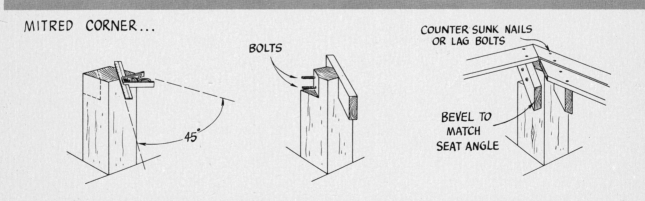

45°

BOLTS

COUNTER SUNK NAILS
OR LAG BOLTS

BEVEL TO
MATCH
SEAT ANGLE

DOUBLE POST ASSEMBLY...

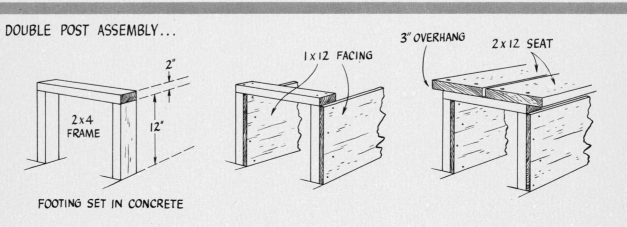

2"

2 x 4
FRAME

12"

FOOTING SET IN CONCRETE

1 x 12 FACING

3" OVERHANG

2 x 12 SEAT

1. Build it solidly so it will take abuse and won't come apart if the soil shifts in winter. Use bolts or lag screws and concealed braces for good measure.

2. Sink posts at least 18 inches into the soil, and encase them in concrete so they won't get the wobbles. Treat posts with pentachlorophenol or copper or zinc naphthenate for long life.

3. Seat walls that are to double as retainers for planting beds should be treated throughout with preservative.

4. Place the seat at chair level. The standard is 16 inches. You can go higher than this by a few inches, but a lower level is likely to be uncomfortable for everyone but your children.

5. Place posts a maximum of 5 feet apart to avoid sag in the bench planks.

6. Use only top grade redwood, cedar, or cypress for the seat planks that are exposed to weathering. Select knot-free pieces if you can get them so there will be no danger of pitch stains on clothes.

7. To prevent other damage to clothes, plane and sandpaper all edges to remove splinters, and repeat periodically. Countersink nails and boltheads in the seat. Use aluminum or zinc coated nails to avoid rust stains. Paint with a wood stain that does not contain oils that will work out.

8. For comfort, provide kick space beneath the seat. If your bench is enclosed below the seat, set the siding back from the edge to allow plenty of room for heels.

9. Although a single plank, such as 2x12, looks more solid than 3 2x4's or 2 2x6's, it is more likely to warp. Set the narrower boards with a little clearance to allow rain water to drain through.

CURVED BENCHES

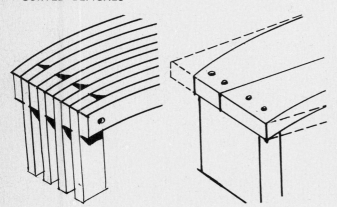

There are two ways to build a curved bench. It may be formed from two wide planks, cut to match the curve, or by laminating a set of narrow strips, as shown in the drawing. The second method is probably sturdier, but it is sometimes uncomfortable to sit upon.

Osmundson-Staley, Design and Photo

Redwood seat wall is gray stained, used as garden accent to contrast flat lawn. Verticals are 3x6's, spaced 3 feet apart

Eckbo, Royston & Williams, Design; Ron Partridge Photo

Seat carefully mitered at corners to give effect of continuous line. White-painted seat of 2x6's supported on 4x4 posts

Eckbo, Royston & Williams, Design; Ernest Braun, Photo

Curved seat wall made of 1x2-inch redwood strips, supported on arms cantilevered out from curved grapestake fence behind

Concrete block wall with hollows used as plant pockets. Raised bed also of concrete block, wood capped for seat

CONCRETE BLOCKS . . . economical and quickly assembled

A sturdy and economical wall can be built in a hurry with concrete blocks. The big blocks (8x8x16 inches) make the wall seem to come together like magic.

Some people object to the material, considering it too cold and commercial for garden use. The fact that it is used widely for stores, factories, and warehouses gives some support to this objection. But a wall of this material need not be cold and forbidding, if the designer uses the material carefully. The porous-surfaced blocks provide an interesting garden texture; large blocks may be combined with

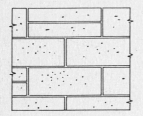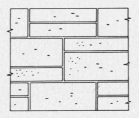

smaller ones to give the effect of fitted stonework; or the whole surface may be covered with stucco,

Large concrete blocks used for three walls: tree box, raised bed and 9-foot wall that supports the overhead lath sunscreen

colored with masonry paint.

Two types of concrete block are used for building walls. One is made from the same materials as regular concrete; the other is made with pumice or cinders substituted for the gravel aggregates. Marketed under various trade names, the second variety is generally known as pumice block.

The regular concrete blocks are heavier than the pumice—an 8x8x16 concrete block weighs about 50 pounds, the pumice about 27 pounds. Pumice blocks are less tiring to lay up, and they may be drilled, nailed, or sawed with a mason's saw. Concrete blocks are more water-resistant than the lighter blocks, however, and are better suited to foundation courses or retaining walls where moisture is a factor.

Concrete blocks are obtainable in a bewildering assortment of sizes and shapes, developed by the industry to meet every conceivable need in building construction. Fortunately, the garden wall-builder can get by with only one or two sizes, such as the popular 8x8x16 or the smaller 4x8x16. Some of the sizes are shown below.

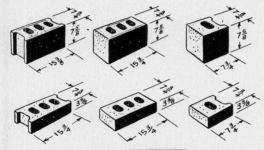

LAYING UP THE WALL

Technique for laying up concrete blocks is generally similar to laying clay bricks, as described in the chapter on that subject.

Concrete block walls should be erected on a substantial footing of poured concrete.

First step is to set the first course in place without mortar and shift the blocks around slightly until they fit. This process, known as "running out the bond," may save your having to cut a block. You may find that you will need to fill out the course with a half-block, a standard unit obtainable from your dealer. Try to keep the spaces between the blocks no wider than ½ inch, no narrower than ¼ inch. When you are satisfied with the line-up, mark the foundation to show the position of each block, and put them aside.

Mix your mortar to a formula of 1:1:3, as described in the chapter on laying brick walls.

Clean off the concrete foundation and wet it down. Trowel on a patch of mortar, just large enough to seat the first block. Place a dry block on it and tap it with the trowel handle to give it a firm bedding. Trowel enough mortar alongside for the next block, butter the end of the first one, and fit the new block in place.

For the next course, trowel the mortar in strips along the outside edge of the top of the course just laid. Put down just enough for one block at a time. It is not necessary to butter the partitions, or "webs," between the hollow spaces, nor is it necessary to fill in the latter. Stand the next block on one

Low wall of concrete blocks is capped with peaked mortar coping to shed rainwater, keep it from penetrating masonry

Severity of plain concrete block wall is relieved by openwork, formed by laying blocks on their sides to form design

Painted concrete block wall supports arbor. Pipe, 3½ inches, welded to arbor frame. Cotoneaster espalier nailed to blocks

Bleakness of 6-foot wall relieved by espaliered pyracantha, planted in tubs made from three concrete tree rings, mortared

Concrete block walls, one supporting raised bed, other for 6-foot boundary along the street, enhance pleasant terrace

end and butter mortar on the other. Pick it up, bump it against a solid surface to seat the mortar, then put it in place in the wall.

Vertical reinforcing rods are not required unless the wall must withstand strong wind or soil pressure. If needed, set them in grout, 32 inches on center.

When you lay the top course, seal it from water penetration. Fill in the hollow spaces solidly with mortar and trowel a smooth layer along the top to receive the coping. Coping may be wood, bricks, or concrete block veneer.

Joints should be struck smooth after the mortar has stiffened.

PAINTING

Portland cement paint provides the most lasting and weatherproof surface coating. It should not be applied sooner than 24 days after the wall is finished, nor should it be attempted when temperature is below 40° or if there is frost in the masonry. Painting should preferably be done in the shade. The two-coat operation is carried out as follows:

1. Clean surface of oil, grease, dirt, and dust; remove efflorescence with 20 percent solution of muriatic acid; fill in small cracks with thick paste of the cement paint.

2. Mix paint in accordance with manufacturer's instructions.

3. Dampen the surface thoroughly with the garden hand spray.

4. When surface water no longer is visible, brush on paint with a coarse-bristled brush, such as a scrub or fender brush.

5. Paint mortar joints first and *scrub* paint into the blocks for good penetration. Keep wet for 24 hours.

6. Not sooner than 24 hours after applying the first coat, brush on the finish coat. Try to cover the whole wall in one operation, or at least carry it to a natural stopping point.

7. Keep the finish coat damp for 48 hours. Protect it from wind, heat, and strong sunshine to permit full curing of the paint.

Curving brick wall is structurally strong as well as graceful in appearance. Retainer is 8 inches thick, seat wall 12 inches

BRICKS . . . handyman's favorite

Most home handymen serve their apprenticeship as amateur bricklayers by trying brick paving projects first. It is only after they develop more confidence by handling the material that they move on to the next stage—building walls and other vertical structures.

In the long run, it is wise not to be in too much of a hurry with these projects. Do your preliminary figuring carefully. Study and practice the bricklaying techniques.

THICKNESS OF WALLS

Walls 4 inches thick (the width of one brick) are adequate if they don't go more than a foot or two high and don't have to withstand much lateral pressure or lateral shocks.

Exception is the curved or serpentine wall. A curved wall forms its own support, and can be built without pilasters, and is stronger than a straight wall. To lay one out, handle each curve as a part of the circumference of a circle. Set up a stake or pole the right distance away and swing from it a line or board to guide you. Another possibility is to make

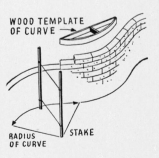

up a wooden template. A most important requirement is to make the curve (or curves) pleasing to the eye.

(13)

Wall gains color and pattern from mortar-streaked used bricks and dark clinker brick. Lily pool octagonal in shape

Low wall for raised bed is broadened out to serve as seat wall. Built of used bricks, mortared cap; note mowing strip

Lead-in wall from highway built of whitewashed bricks. Second from top course laid on edge, slanted at 45 degree angle

Higher walls and retaining walls are better made 8 or more inches thick, with steel reinforcing rods in mortar joints at frequent intervals.

Using a rolok bond you can save bricks without sacrificing strength in an 8-inch wall. In any reference book on bricklaying you can find others, based on different combinations of headers (crosswise) and stretchers (lengthwise).

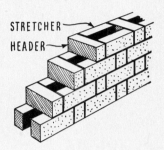

When you build large walls, you have to be especially careful about reinforcement. A long, high brick wall should be reinforced about every 12 feet with a pilaster or brick pier.

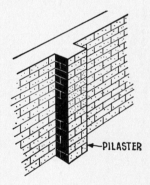

Grout-lock, or *Keybrick* (illustrated), makes a good wall. Lay it up like ordinary brick, then pour grout (thin, soupy mortar) into the hollow interior of the wall.

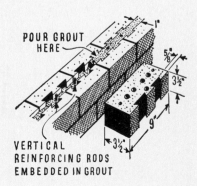

If you plan to cap a wall with a redwood plank put threaded bolts at intervals in the mortar joints when you lay the last course. Let them protrude exactly the right amount, or plan to cut them off later, so that the nut can be recessed in the wood.

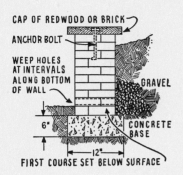

CAP OF REDWOOD OR BRICK

ANCHOR BOLT

WEEP HOLES
AT INTERVALS
ALONG BOTTOM
OF WALL

GRAVEL

CONCRETE
BASE

6"

12"

FIRST COURSE SET BELOW SURFACE

MORTAR

Mortar is a mixture of cement, fine sand, and water with a small amount of lime or fireclay added for plasticity.

Formula: There are dozens of mortar mixes, each with its stanch advocate in and out of the bricklaying trade. For garden masonry, you'll find the standard Type B Mortar (Uniform Building Code) to be a good all-purpose mix. Here are the proportions:

2 parts Portland cement.
1 part fireclay or hydrated lime.
9 parts graded sand.

The fireclay or lime make the mortar spread easily; the choice between them is largely a matter of personal preference. Some bricklayers prefer lime putty to hydrated lime. It is a mixture of lime, water, and usually a little sand, in a plastic state. Some building supply dealers sell it in bulk.

Sand should be "sharp," made up of angular particles, free of dirt. If you wet it and squeeze it, it should not bind together and should not leave a slimy deposit in the hand. If you can't get a special mortar sand, a 50-50 mix of fine concrete sand and plaster sand will do.

Avoid Too Much Sand. This makes the mortar short. It won't hang to the trowel or the brick, and you'll have a hard time making smoothly tooled joints.

Estimating Quantity: Materials needed per 100 square feet of wall surface, using "Type B" mortar with half-inch joints:

	4-inch wall	8-inch wall
Bricks	550	1100
Cement	2 cu. ft.	4½ cu. ft.
Lime	1 cu. ft.	2½ cu. ft.
Sand	9 cu. ft.	20 cu. ft.

Mason Weymouth, Photo

Open grid relieves heaviness of 7½-foot brick wall and repeats design of house window framing; built of used bricks

Philip Fein, Photo

Six-foot garden wall built of used, irregular shaped bricks, painted white. Deep mortar joints emphasize shadow pattern

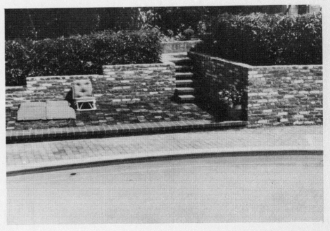

Thomas Church, Design and Photo

Used bricks in wall break up its flatness and give color to contrast with smooth sheen of water in swimming pool

Thomas Church, Design and Photo

Raised bed used with wall seems, optically, to reduce height of wall and ties wall and flower bed together as one unit

Bob Holdeman, Design; William C. Aplin, Photo

Combination of seat wall and plant box built with bricks laid on edge. The surface of the seat half is laid over a fill

Richard J. Neutra, Design; Julius Shulman, Photo

Wall, paving, and circular pool smoothly connected with house. Top of the 12-inch wall is recessed for planting box

Mortar ingredients figured to the nearest ½ cubic foot, allowing for reasonable waste. Sack of cement (100 pounds), sack of lime (50 pounds) or fireclay (80 lbs.), and sack of sand (100 pounds) each equals approximately one cubic foot.

Mixing: You can use almost any flat surface for mixing mortar: a small platform made of 1x4's laid close together, an old wheelbarrow, a wooden box, a square of plywood. Mix it in small batches so it won't dry out. Here is a reasonable amount to try, sufficient for about 50 bricks:

> 1 shovelful of cement.
> 4½ shovelfuls of sand.
> ½ shovelful of fireclay or lime.

Mix the ingredients thoroughly in their dry state with a hoe. Scoop out a hollow, add water, and mix carefully. Continue blending and adding water until the mortar slips cleanly off the blade of the hoe. If a batch starts to dry out while in use, freshen it with a small amount of water. Use it up within an hour.

LAYING BRICK

Tools and Equipment: To be a bricklayer, you will need a few tools. Two of them will come right out of the mason's tool bag: a sturdy, pointed trowel with a 10-inch blade, for buttering mortar, and a broad-bladed cold chisel known as a "brick set," for cutting bricks. Other tools will come from your

TROWEL HAMMER BRICK SET COLD CHISEL

workshop: a hammer, a 2-foot spirit level, a carpenter's square, a stretch of old fishing line. You will also need a piece of straight wood 4 or 5 feet long. If you want to attempt a truly professional-looking job, you may wish to invest in additional mason's paraphernalia, such as a pointing trowel and a jointer or two.

Common bricks should be damp, but not wet, when they are laid. When they are too wet, they dilute the mortar and cause it to run, and they slip in the mortar bed. If you plan to work on your wall in the morning, let a very fine spray play over the brick pile for the last hour and a half of the afternoon before. For bricks you are going to lay in the afternoon, start this process in the morning about 4 hours before you plan to use them.

Before you start mortaring the bricks in place, experiment with lining them up dry to check on your measurements. String a loose row of them on top of the foundation. If the bricks seem to fill to your guide lines properly, with ½ inch open between each brick for the mortar joint, then start setting them in for good.

Setting Bricks in Mortar: A professional places his equipment about like this:

MORTAR BOARD

The mortar board is just a small platform about two feet square. A good substitute is the top surface of an orange crate stood on end.

He reaches his trowel out to the mortar board on his right and cuts down into the mortar as if he were cutting a cake, pulling enough toward him to handle three or four bricks. (If you are a beginner, better start with enough for one brick.)

As he gets the mortar out to the edge, he scoops up the trowelful quickly and swings it with a straight-arm motion over to the wall at his left. He usually works along a wall from left to right. He

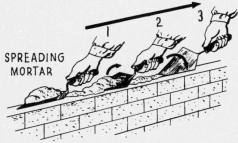

SPREADING MORTAR

spreads the mortar over the top course of brick, gradually turning the trowel toward him until the

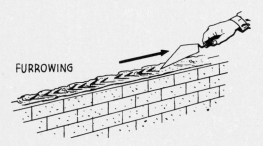

FURROWING

Eckbo, Royston & Williams, Design; William C. Aplin, Photo

Freestanding plant box for display of trailing vines and plants; first shelf is for pots, the second contains soil pocket

Maynard Parker, Photo

Planting boxes of 5-course, 8-inch brickwork, harmonize with brick-in-sand terrace, provide easily-cared-for beds

Thomas Church, Design and Photo

Plants in bloom behind seat wall are visible above it; but during off-season, the wall becomes the visual limit of garden

Andrew Gotzenburg, Design

Solid structure in appearance and actuality, yet repetition of brick in the wall, steps, and walk is not monotonous

William Penn Mott, Design; Howard Hoffman, Photo

Eight-inch brick wall used for retaining wall, plant box, and a freestanding boundary wall in this pleasant sun terrace

Cortland Van Horn, Design; Robert C. Cleveland, Photo

All-ceramic outdoor room in a natural woodland setting; brick wall, fireplace, barbecue; tile paving, counter tops

blade is perpendicular as he finishes. Then he comes back across this mortar bed with the point of his trowel and lightly "furrows" (gouges) it in a zig-zag line to push it out approximately even with the edge of the brick. He trims off the edge of the mortar bed, lays a brick in place with his left hand, trims off excess mortar again, and uses this to butter the end of the next brick, and so on until he has to go back for more mortar.

It is extremely difficult, but worthwhile, to set your brick right the first time, so you don't have to slide it or tap it into place. The mortar will set better and your work will move faster.

Build up the ends or corners of a wall first, in steps. You will need them as leads for your line. You may need to step up additional leads in the middle if the wall is long. Use a plumb level—or any level that can be used vertically—and a 4-foot straight-edge of wood to keep ends plumb.

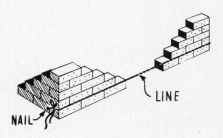

Use a strong guide line. A good quality fish line is satisfactory. You can use nails to anchor the ends. Put them into mortar joints, filling in the holes as you move up course by course. Over a long span, you can keep the line from sagging by using what the bricklayer calls a *"trig,"* a loose brick laid on top of the last course with a string tied around it and the line.

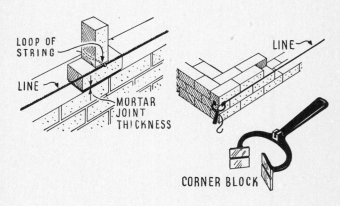

With *corner blocks* you can avoid putting holes in the mortar joints. You can buy a pair in a hardware store, or you can make up corner blocks of your own.

STRIKING MORTAR JOINTS

Now for the finishing touches. Just before the mortar sets, trim off any loose or extruded bits, and smooth off the joints. Dress the vertical ones first, then the horizontal. You may use your trowel for this operation, but you will find it much simpler to use a short piece of pipe that is slightly larger than the width of the joint—a ¾-inch water pipe is fine for a ½-inch joint. By drawing the pipe along the mortar joint, you can produce a smooth, concave surface. A short, rounded stick will do just as well.

For a professional-looking finish, you can finish the joints in one of these three popular ways: Style A can be made with the edge of a board; style B

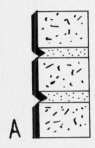 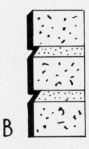 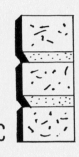

with the handle of the trowel held down; and style C with the handle of the trowel held up. The B joint is preferred because of its water-shedding ability and the fact that each course of bricks will throw a horizontal line of shadow along the wall.

CLEAN-UP

Two or three weeks after you have completed the job, you can clean up any random smears of mortar or traces of the white efflorescence that often appears on fresh brickwork, by applying a mild solution of muriatic acid. This is a potent chemical that should be handled with respect. In its raw state it will dissolve concrete, and even in diluted form it will eat through paint, galvanized pails, and clothing. If it spills, it should be flushed off at once with plenty of water. For use on masonry, mix 10 parts of water with 1 part of acid in a wide-mouth glass jar, pouring the acid into the water and stirring with a stick. Apply it with an old rag, and when you have finished the entire surface of the wall, wash it off thoroughly with the hose. If any of the solution comes in contact with your skin, rinse it off, then wash with a solution of bicarbonate of soda.

Incidentally, mortar itself can shrivel the skin on your fingers to a disconcerting degree. No need for alarm, though. It draws the natural oils out of the skin, but they can be restored by rubbing in hand lotion or vaseline.

John Yeon, Design

A distinguished wall of fine texture and intricate masonry is mirrored in lily pool. Half-roman bricks are used in wall

Eckbo, Royston & Williams, Design; William C. Aplin, Photo

Openwork in brick designed for more than decoration, for it permits the part of the garden on other side to be seen

Strong but graceful lines of dressed stone wall prove that stonework need not be heavy and clumsy if it is properly designed

STONE . . . challenge to craftsmanship

A stonemason will warn you against trying to build a stone wall yourself. He will contend that rock-work is an exacting craft, and that although an amateur *can* build a handsome wall he is just as likely to create a monstrosity.

Compared with brickwork, stonecraft is difficult. There is more weight to handle, the uneven surfaces make plumb lines difficult to achieve, and the individual stones are hard to cut and shape. Setting heavy rocks in place is no child's game. The heavy stones squash the mortar bed, jam in wrong positions, or just refuse to fit in. Par on barked knuckles is higher for rock than for brickwork.

But don't let these minor obstacles scare you away from building a wall of stone. If you respond to a challenging material—and have plenty of rocks close at hand—you will find stonecraft a rewarding project. A carefully fitted stone wall has an honest beauty that few other materials can match.

Stone walls can be built either with or without mortar. If you follow a few simple rules, you should have no difficulty with either method.

KINDS TO USE

Almost any kind of stone that is available in quantity may be used, although some types are more

Natural stones fitted together with unbelievably thin joints show the master touch of a skilled stoneworker

satisfactory than others.

The easiest stones to trim and face are the *stratified* rocks, such as limestone, shale, and sandstone. As their name implies, they are formed of layers of solidified soil deposit, a property that makes some of them easy to split and chip. However, they have a serious flaw that restricts their value in severe climates: extreme cold will make them come apart at the seams. In winter, they will absorb moisture and then split open when it turns to ice during a freezing spell. However, if you want to build your wall of stratified stone, you can overcome this unfortunate trait. If you trowel in your mortar solidly to prevent water from infiltrating and if you apply a good masonry sealer a few months after the job is done your wall should weather many a hostile winter.

The most durable rocks are the tough old granites and basalts. Their very toughness, though, makes them an obstinate material to handle. They are hard to break and chip; in fact, an amateur is likely to injure himself in attempting it. They are also slow to lay up, because they absorb so little water from the mortar that they delay its drying time.

TYPES OF STONEWORK

Stonework is divided into two broad classes, *rubble* and *ashlar*. Rubble masonry is composed of uncut stones, fitted into the structure in their natural state. Ashlar masonry is built with cut stones, laid in fairly regular courses. Unstratified stones are often set in rubble form because they are so difficult and expensive to cut; and layered rocks are usually found in ashlar work, because they are easily dressed by the quarryman's saws and cutters.

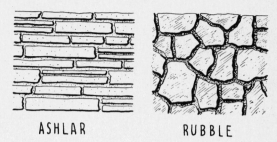

ASHLAR   RUBBLE

A wall can be built with either cut or uncut stones. An amateur may find ashlar easier than rubble, because the shaped stones can be set in place with less juggling than the rounded and irregular field stones. However, dressed stones are usually more costly.

STONEWORK PATTERNS

The irregular sizes, shapes, and colors of stone give the stoneworker free range in design, and it is often because of this that the amateur comes up with a "monsterpiece." If properly placed, stones should produce harmonious and pleasing patterns in which there is variety but good composition. The finished structure should appear to be a unit rather than a conglomeration of rocks.

Here are some ways of insuring good, solid design:

1. The individual stones should be laid as they would lie naturally on the ground. They should rarely be placed on end or in unnatural positions.

Thomas Church, Design and Photo

Stones laid in mortar for structural strength, but while the mortar is wet, dirt put in joints to give effect of dry wall

Walter and Florence Gerke, Design; Charles Pearson, Photo

Small lily pool gives interest to corner of seat wall. Built of carefully fitted cut stone. Pool is waterproofed inside

2. Continuous wavy joints between stones should be avoided where the resulting "lightning bolt" pattern will destroy the feeling of strength and solidity inherent in all good stonework.

3. Large stones should be laid in the lower courses, small stones in the upper. This does not mean that small stones should be used *only* in the upper sections, but a larger proportion of the more solid rock is used in the base courses.

4. Stones of the same size or shape should not be set side by side. Avoid "peanut brittle" effect by setting in a long, narrow stone or one that is much larger than the adjacent rocks.

5. A strong wall requires "bonding"—the overlapping of two small stones by one long one.

TOOLS AND EQUIPMENT

Tools needed are: a hammer, preferably a waller's or mason's hammer; a sledge hammer if large stones are to be broken; an old tub or wooden box for holding the mortar. For the foundation work, a spade and shovel will be required, and a wheelbarrow should be on hand for carrying materials around on the job.

For spreading mortar, use a regular brick trowel. In order to keep the work aligned, mason's twine can be used, stretched taut to mark the boundaries of the wall or structure. Use a level for checking alignment as the work goes on. Keep several smooth, straight boards on hand for making angles for checking the inclination — *batter* — of the wall. An old broom, with the bristles trimmed, will make an excellent brush with which to clean the work of excess

mortar before it has set. Other tools found around the house—hoe, sprinkler, hose, etc.—will be useful as the work progresses.

QUANTITY OF STONE REQUIRED

Estimates of the amount of stone required for masonry work are usually figured in tons. The area that a ton will occupy depends, of course, on the type of stone used. For example, a ton of fieldstone will fill from 25 to 40 *cubic* feet of wall; while a ton of dressed flagstone, laid as veneer, will cover 55 *square* feet. In some localities, stone is sold by the cubic yard (27 cu. ft.), which will occupy slightly more than the same volume of wall. Your dealer is accustomed to figuring these quantities. If you provide him with the total cubic wall area in your wall, he will compute the amount of rock needed.

When selecting stones, choose a variety of sizes, keeping in mind the scale of the work. A good rule to remember is that the face area of the larger stones laid should not be more than 5 or 6 times the face area of the smallest stones. Large stones, of course, can sometimes be broken to size while the work is progressing. If you plan to use cut stone, order specific thicknesses and designate the upper and lower limits of length. Here, again, the longer slabs may be broken on the job.

MORTAR

Rockwork requires a relatively large quantity of mortar, because of the irregular size of the mortar joints and the numerous voids that have to be filled

John Robinson, Photo

Stones should lie in wall as though stable, set against upheaval; not in unnatural on-edge positions that defy gravity

John Robinson, Photo

Don't lay stones in place so they appear to be emerging from a doughy mass. Wall strength depends on stone, not mortar

in. A structure built of fieldstone or river rock, for instance, may contain as much as a third of its volume in mortar.

Estimating the amount needed in a wall is largely inspired guesswork. One fairly sure way of working out the problem is to lay up a small section, figure the amount of mortar used, then compute the quantity needed for the rest of the wall and order accordingly. However, a surer way than this is to pass the whole problem over to your dealer, who can be relied upon to figure it out correctly.

Formula: The formula recommended for rock mortar is richer than for brick:

> 1 part cement.
> 3 parts clean sand
> ½ part fireclay.

Do not use hydrated lime in place of fireclay because it is likely to discolor the stones.

Mixing: See instructions on mortar mixing in the chapter on brickwork.

FOUNDATION

For strength, the foundation of any masonry structure should be built of stone or concrete *well below* the surface of the ground. Where winters are mild (foundation should go down below frost level), 10 to 12 inches (for a 3-foot wall) is sufficient depth for the trench in which the stone is laid or the concrete is poured. The bottom of the trench should be on firm ground; do not place the foundation upon filled ground.

Start the actual masonry structure, if concrete is used, a little below the surface of the ground and lay it directly, with mortar, on the foundation of concrete.

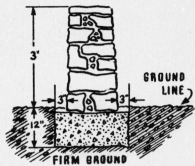

For a foundation, concrete is easy to lay and, usually where stone is not readily available, is cheaper. When stone is used for the foundation, it should be laid with mortar, solidly in the trench.

SETTING STONEWORK

Following are some recommendations to guide you in building with stone:

1. Have plenty of rock handy. If you have a choice of sizes and shapes, you will not be inclined to force the job. Place the stones where you can reach them as you work. To keep your pattern interesting and insure good bonding, try several rocks in a section of the wall before mortaring.

2. All stones should be cleaned thoroughly. Remove all dirt and lichen from surfaces to be mor-

Jerry Anson, Photo

Don't make wall a potpourri of rock varieties; keep shapes, colors, textures matched; only enough variety for interest

Jerry Anson, Photo

Carefully fitted sandstone in ashlar bond. The wall gains in strength by placement of large stones and long stretchers

Howard Hoffman, Photo

Appearance and strength of dry wall of square-cut stones would have been improved by setting large stones along base

Thomas Church, Design and Photo

Pair of dry walls restrain hillside and also provide planting beds. The stones are slanted toward the hillside for stability

John Robinson, Photo

Old-fashioned stone fence corral, a by-product of clearing fields. Requires a lot of space and stone, but lasts forever

tared. Do not brush with an iron bristle-brush as this may produce latent rust stains. If you clean the stones with water, let them dry before mortaring.

3. String guide lines and keep the face of the structure flush by selecting rocks and setting them so they do not jut beyond the face of the wall.

4. To give the wall the proper "batter," or slope nail two boards together (as illustrated) at the angle desired. A regular wall should slope 1 inch in every

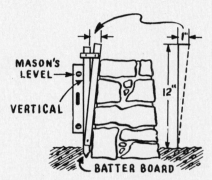

24 inches of height. A retaining wall, 1 inch in every 12. Use the angle board as the work progresses. Don't rely altogether on the mason's twine.

5. Be sure the joints are properly bonded by overlapping the vertical joints at every course. Put in headers—stones set with their long dimensions at right angles to the face of the wall—to strengthen the wall transversely.

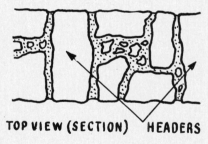

6. Use enough mortar to fill *completely* all the joints. Make the joints as thin as possible. Chink with small chips of stone, all empty spaces between rocks in the interior of the wall, and fill with mortar.

7. If you have to shift a stone that is already set in mortar, lift it clear of the mortar bed, scrape off all mortar, and replace with a fresh layer.

8. After you have laid one section, rake out the joints on the facing before the mortar sets. Use a stick with a dull point. The rake should be ½ to ¾ of an inch—the deeper the rake, the better the shadow effect. Thoroughly brush off all excess mortar with an old broom before it has set too firmly.

9. If it is necessary to touch up—point—joints after the mortar has hardened, do it very carefully with a pointing mixture of one part sand to one part cement with a little fireclay added.

DRY WALL

A dry wall—one that is assembled without mortar—is a challenging and attractive form of stonework. The stones are carefully fitted together in mosaic fashion so they hold each other in place by weight and friction.

Freestanding Wall: A freestanding wall is built without deep foundation—even in regions of severe climate. It may topple or list as a result of frost action, but it is easily repaired in the spring. Custom calls for bedding the foundation course below grade—not below frost level—or even on the surface of the soil. Base stones should be larger than those used in the wall and may be mortared in place for a level bed.

The wall is held together by the bond stones that pass through it. One should be placed for every 10 square feet of wall surface (about 1 every 3 feet, every third course). Corners and ends should be almost entirely bond stone construction. Gate posts require mortared joints. The top course should be laid as level as possible; save your flattest stones for it.

Retaining Walls: A well constructed dry wall can serve as an effective and distinctive retainer.

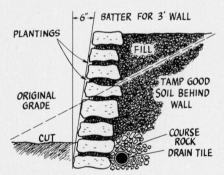

Stones should be placed so the back ends tip down into the ground, and their front faces, when seen in profile, slant slightly upward. Backward slanting of the wall provides stronger resistance against pressure from the earth behind, and allows moisture to penetrate. Steeper the bank, greater the slope to the wall.

Use largest stones in the lower course for the most part. High, steep walls need large stones throughout. If no large stones available for upper courses, use smaller ones and step the wall back a little to form a slight shelf or recession before continuing with the next course.

If plants are to be grown in the wall, they should be planted when the wall is built. Roots can be spread out in natural growing position and larger plants can be used than when the wall is finished. A mixture of topsoil, leaf mold, and well-rotted manure should be rammed into the space behind the wall as it is built. Use the same mixture in crevices between stones so plants will take hold easily.

Howard Gilkey & Floyd Cowan, Design; John Robinson, Photo

Walls of dressed stone provide planting bed, pool, patio support. Glass windscreen in steel sash mortared to wall

Rugged steps in dry stone wall made of single slabs of dressed stone. They are heavy to put in place, but are stable, durable

John Robinson, Photo

Dressed sandstone laid like brick. Material easy to lay but difficult to prevent staining it with mortar. Needs waterseal

Geraldine Knight Scott, Design; Mason Weymouth, Photo

Generous size of adobe blocks in scale with the large oaks and wide open garden. Bright plants accent against adobe

ADOBE BLOCKS . . . weight without heaviness

A wall built of adobe blocks has an air of substantial informality about it. Although heavy and solid-looking, its earthy color and irregular textures make it seem less forbidding than other masonry walls. It seems somehow to be more obviously a product of the human hand than a wall of poured concrete, concrete blocks, or even bricks. There are people behind this wall, it seems to say, not machines.

Somewhat overpowering when used in a confined area, an adobe wall looks its best when enclosing a free and open garden plan, where large trees and open vistas predominate. The generous size of the blocks seem in scale with trees and spreading space; and from a distance, the texture of the wall can still be seen and understood.

When left its natural color, adobe harmonizes with the warm tones of redwood or cedar house trim; when painted, it matches more formal exteriors, but the rough surface prevents the wall from becoming bleak and unfriendly.

SETTING ADOBE BLOCKS

The method of laying adobe blocks is similar to that for laying up a brick wall, as described in the chapter on that subject.

Principal difference, of course, is the size of the bricks. The adobe blocks usually laid in walls run 4x8x16 inches, the equivalent of 4 or 5 clay bricks. One advantage of the large size is that the blocks make a wall go together rapidly.

When you lay up an adobe wall, you soon become painfully aware of the weight you are handling. Toward the end of the day, the 30-pound blocks begin to feel double their weight, particularly when you start setting them at chest height. They are hard to shift around once they are laid in place, so you have to develop a knack for placing them in the right spot to begin with.

You will find it easier if you can persuade someone to help you, so you can trade off tasks. One can be mixing mortar or wheeling blocks from the stack while the other lays bricks; and after a while, you switch jobs.

An adobe wall requires a sturdy foundation. The heavy blocks are not so shock-resistant as clay bricks. This is only natural, for a puddled material such as adobe doesn't have the same strength as kiln-fired clay. Sometimes the mortar that binds the wall together is stronger than the blocks them-

1. Adobe blocks are stacked in slanted piles so they won't topple over, will shed rainwater, and be easier to pick up

2. The mortar is first applied roughly, enough for several blocks, then is smoothed out to level bed with mason's trowel

3. Heavy blocks seem heavier as wall rises. Must be put in place without much shifting around. Aligned with guide string

4. For smooth surface, joints are struck with steel float instead of pointing trowel when mortar has set up slightly

5. Steel reinforcing rods are needed to prevent the corner from parting, add strength to wall. Placed every third course

6. Gates are attached to wall by mortaring hinge-pin assembly in joints. Design of the hinge bracket prevents twisting

If properly designed and braced, stabilized adobe blocks make a sturdy retaining wall. These walls are 3 feet high

Walls and steps of adobe block matched with redwood house. Thick joints, roughly struck give informal air to the wall

Painted adobe wall, 5 feet high, encloses pleasant patio entrance to adobe house, seems integral part of structure

selves. As a consequence, an adobe wall must have a solid foundation that won't yield to soil movement, and lateral steel reinforcement (⅜ bar) is needed every third course. Reinforcement is also essential at corners to anchor the two stretches of wall to each other.

Mortar: Mortar is richer than that required for clay bricks. Formula is:

Portland cement	1	part
Sand	2½	parts
Stabilizer (to sack of cement)	1½	gals.

Dirt can be added to mortar for color in a ratio of 2 parts to every 3 of sand.

Adobe blocks should be laid dry, kept covered during rain.

Materials Needed: For 100 square feet of wall, with ¾-inch mortar joints, you will need:

Adobe blocks	200
Sand (cu. ft.)	9
Portland cement (sacks)	3½
Stabilizer (gallons)	3½

Amount of reinforcing steel would depend upon height of the wall and the number of courses. On an average, 100 square feet of 6-foot wall would require 320 pounds. Walls, lower than 4 feet do not require steel reinforcement.

PAINTING AND STUCCOING

If the architectural plan calls for painting the adobe or applying a coating of stucco, you had better call in a local painting expert who can come out and examine the adobes. Variation between batches of adobe bricks is such that usually a spot analysis is advisable before any paint is bought. Ordinary masonry paints will not prevent the asphalt stabilizer from bleeding through.

Design of this adobe boundary wall makes it seem lighter because of graceful curve and openings left between blocks

Thomas Church, Design   Philip Fein, Photo

A poured concrete wall can be shaped to any curve or angle or painted any color needed to realize the landscaping plan

POURED CONCRETE . . . strength with freedom of form

Poured concrete has many advantages as a material for building a garden wall. A poured wall can be formed into almost any shape to fit the garden plan, for it does not have to be erected on a straightaway and can be shaped to any curve or angle. Its surface texture can be finished smooth, rough, or embossed with architectural lines. Its tough, durable qualities recommend it for holding back a hillside or containing a planting bed. Unlike a concrete slab, a concrete wall can be easily colored.

But pouring a concrete wall is no Sunday picnic for the handyman. Even the simplest job calls for carefully fitted and strongly built forms to hold the concrete while it cures. If a wall is curved or sharply angled, its forming requires know-how and skill; and if the wall is a tall one, say 6 feet, the forms must be stanchly braced so they can resist the pressure of the wet concrete without collapsing. Construction of a 6-foot wall also requires an elaborate structure of platforms, ramps, and staging to permit loaded wheelbarrows to be rolled to the top of the forms and dumped. Construction of high walls or those requiring complex forming are best entrusted to a reliable contractor.

However, an amateur can readily handle a simple low wall, such as a seat wall or the edge of a raised bed. Forms for a low wall are not difficult to build, and they are easily filled with concrete. The wet mix can be dumped into the forms from a wheelbarrow with its wheel resting on the ground or on a plank ramp, or from the drum of the mixer if it is stationed close by, or, if the handyman can assemble all his relatives and friends, he may be able to fill his wall in one fell swoop with a load of transit-mix. With good luck, an amateur can even cast a modest curve.

FORMING

Building and aligning the forms takes more time than the actual pouring of the concrete. You may devote four or five weekends to form building and only one to filling them with concrete. Here are the important points to remember:

1. Provide a suitable foundation by digging down to firm hard ground or below frost level in severe climates. Dig out the foundation trench 4 inches wider than the wall. As the average low wall is 6 inches wide, a 10-inch trench would thus be needed.

2. Build double-walled forms from lumber that is free of knotholes and warpage. Use plywood for a smooth finish. Brace the forms substantially to hold them vertically.

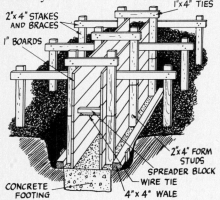

3. To round a curve, use notched lumber. Soak 1x6's or 1x4's, make saw cuts about halfway through on side to be curved inward. Hold in place with secure bracing. Uneven surface of cast wall can be smoothed over with cement paste. Metal may also be used for a smooth, clean curve.

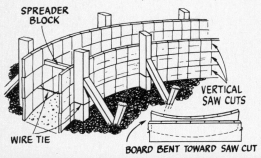

4. Grease forms or brush with crankcase drainings so they will not stick to the concrete. (If you plan to paint the wall, the oil that adheres to the concrete will have to be cleaned off before the paint can be applied. See below.)

5. Place spreaders between boards to hold them against the supporting posts. Fasten a length of wire to each so you can yank it out before pouring concrete around it.

MIXING AND POURING CONCRETE

For description of the technique of mixing concrete, refer to the chapter on concrete paving.

1. Mix to a formula of 1:3:5 or, better, 1:2½:4.

2. Pour in continuous layers 6 to 8 inches deep. Prod and tamp concrete in place with a 2x4 or shovel blade. For a smooth surface, agitate the concrete next to the forms to force the large aggregates away from the surface. Use straight-bladed shovel.

3. If you have to quit work before you finish the wall, cover the top of the concrete with damp sacks and keep them wet until you resume work.

CAPPING

The top surface of a concrete wall should be sealed to keep water from seeping down into it and injuring it during freezing weather.

1. When the wet concrete reaches the top of the forms, float it, let it harden slightly, and then hard-trowel it to a smooth finish. After the cement sets, apply a reliable masonry sealer. Or

2. If the wall is to double as a bench, attach a redwook plank to the top, fastening it to bolts imbedded in the top 3 inches of concrete. Or

Ned Rucker, Design; Philip Fein, Photo

Artful design can overcome bleakness of a tall concrete wall with curving line, decorative coping, and apt planting

Eckbo, Royston & Williams, Design; William C. Aplin, Photo

Free form plant box shows unlimited possibilities of cast concrete. Pebbles set in the concrete reduce its heavy feel

3. If the wall is not going to be used for sitting purposes, add a rounded coping to the top. Trowel a fairly stiff mortar (1:3) on top of the fresh concrete and shape it with a curved template. The round

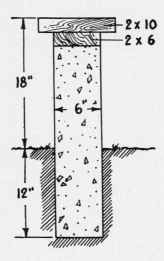

surface will make water run off instead of collecting on top.

CURING

Leave the forms in place for a week after you finish pouring the concrete. Keep only the top surface damp.

If it is necessary to remove the forms while the concrete is still green—say, for broom finishing or integral coloring—cover the entire wall with sacking or tarpaulins and keep it wet for a week.

EXPANSION JOINTS

A freestanding wall that runs longer than 35 feet or one that contains curves or intersecting corners should be provided with expansion joints every 20

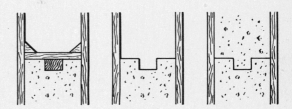

feet to keep it from cracking due to changes in weather. A wall that is exposed to constant sunshine throughout the summer is particularly needful of this precaution. A typical expansion joint is detailed in the drawings.

MATERIALS NEEDED

Materials needed for 100 cubic feet of 6-inch wall are the following:

	1:2½:4	1:3:5
Cement	20 sacks	17 sacks
Sand	2 cu. yds.	2 cu. yds.
Stone	3 cu. yds.	3.5 cu. yds.

PAINTING

Easiest method of coloring a poured wall is to apply Portland cement paint, as described on page 12.

Henry F. Sander, Jr., and Jack L. Laflin, Design; John Robinson, Photo

Low concrete retaining wall is cast in a dramatic curving form. Walk is surfaced with crushed brick in redwood grid

Philip Fein, Photo

Forms for low concrete wall are not difficult to build. A form for seat-height wall is easily filled from wheelbarrow

W. C. Carnack, Design; Philip Fein, Photo

Pair of stepped retaining walls, one of redwood, the other of concrete; plantings on top help protect walls from runoff

RETAINING WALLS . . . remember they're not dams

A little knowledge about retaining walls can be a dangerous thing—so say many building inspectors.

They have good reason for their caution, because they are aware of the forces that a retaining wall sometimes has to retain, and they know what can happen if the wall is not properly engineered and built.

The chief mistake that the innocent builder makes is to erect a dam rather than a wall. During the rainy season, the soil absorbs a large quantity of water which flows downhill below the surface. When this subsurface water reaches an obstruction, such as a wall, it collects and builds up pressure that may finally burst or undermine the wall. If the wall builder makes ample provision to carry ground water through or around his wall, it should stand without trouble.

An amateur can construct a low retaining wall successfully, but if he has any special problems to solve, he should seek professional help. He should not attempt to build the wall without advice if it is taller than 4 feet; if it is to be built on marshy soil, adobe, or fill; or if the slope of the hillside above the wall is greater than 36 percent. Some cities will not issue a building permit for a retaining wall higher than 4 feet unless it is designed, and its construction supervised, by a licensed engineer.

WATER CONTROL

Getting rid of excess water that may take out your wall is sometimes a complex problem. Ditches, gutters, drain tile, and proper planting can be combined to divert the surface floods. Weep holes, tile, and gravel backfill prevent undermining of the wall.

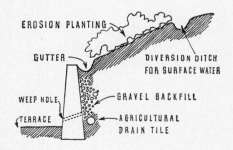

Where weep holes drain water out through a wall, a special gutter may be needed to keep the water from pouring over the lawn or terrace. The gutter should be covered with a grating of wood or metal, and should be pitched slightly to allow run-off water.

Gutter built of planks will handle drainage adequately. Grating can be supported by a cleat on the upright plank, and by a concrete shelf of the wall itself.

Clay tile of the half-hexagonal type can be used, but may be more likely to crack at the angles. Rounded gutters of concrete, shaped when the wall is built, will also serve. Make all gutters shovel-width for cleaning.

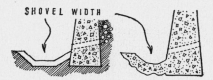

WAYS OF HOLDING THE HILL

It is better to use a series of close-set, low walls than one high wall. Low walls in a series are more pleasing to the eye, easier to plant with vines or shrubs, and less likely to lean or topple down-hill.

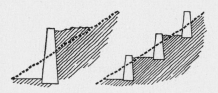

Cast concrete posts, reinforced with wire or rods, make good retaining walls. Anchor them with rods fastened to "deadmen," or use keyed concrete posts run back into the bank. Set plants between posts.

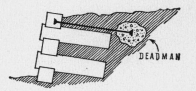

Poured concrete walls should have an extending "foot" on the downhill side, with reinforcement rods curved into the foot.

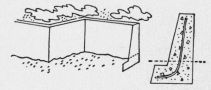

Concrete building blocks, if not laid too many rows high, are good retaining walls. Holes aligned, are filled with cement or heavy pipe to key blocks together.

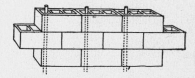

Lewis Baker, Photo

Concrete retaining wall can be built one section at a time. Both rails and arms are precast. Arms extend into hillside, enabling walls to resist pressure of earth. The arm dimensions are shown above. Rails are 5 feet long, 4½ inches square, and are steel reinforced. Two men, working together, can handle. Ground cover plantings will hold the soil and conceal rails

Pierpont, Photo

Brick retaining walls, paired and stepped to form plant boxes. Walls are footed on concrete, reinforced with steel

A. L. Francis, Photo

When steps are built into a retaining wall they must be carefully designed to strengthen and not weaken the wall

Thomas Church, Design and Photo

Carefully fitted dry stonework can make a good retaining wall because it holds back soil but lets water come through

Retaining walls of wood should be built of redwood or cedar, both naturally resistant to rot and insect attacks. However, even these resistant woods should be treated with fungicidal and insect-repellent preservatives. Wall of 4x4's and planks, should have each post braced.

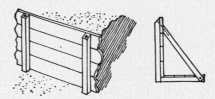

Heavy posts of concrete may be cast at intervals of 6 or 8 feet, reinforced with rods as for concrete walls. Grooves cast into the buttresses hold the ends of treated redwood planks which are slid into place, then back-filled with earth.

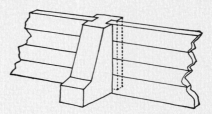

A wall of bricks should not be built to any great height. Even when mortared, bricks do not tie together with the strength of many other retaining-wall materials. Three to 5 feet should be the limit. A solid footing of concrete is necessary. Stagger bricks gradually inward with each course. Use metal rods, attached to sunken concrete "deadmen" in the bank. Leave "weep holes" every 5 feet or so.

Cut-stone walls, the stones laid in mortar, are more sturdy than brick walls because their width is usually greater. Use an angle jig of boards to batter face of wall.

FILL

Dry walls of stone will hold low banks successfully. They can be laid with earth "pockets" between them, then planted with vines or small, shrubby plants. The stones used should be chosen carefully to pitch the wall in toward the thrust of the bank.

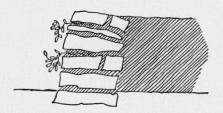

SPECIFICATIONS FOR A TYPICAL WALL

Here are rough specifications for a standard non-reinforced concrete retaining wall.

The top should not be less than 12 inches, regardless of the height, and the base should be 40 to 50 percent of the height. The projecting foot should be about 1/12 the height.

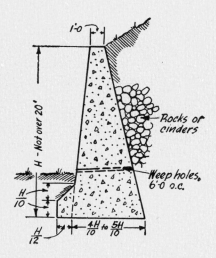

The back of the wall should be sloped from top to bottom in a straight line. (A brick or stone wall may be stepped.)

The footing should be carried below grade at least 18 inches; in frost areas, below the frost level. Weep holes should be set about 6 feet apart, slanted slightly toward the front of the wall, and placed so they drain about 4 inches above ground level. (For walls over 4 feet, a row of weep holes should be placed about every 3 feet in height.)

The back of the wall should be waterproofed with an asphaltic waterproofing compound, applied according to directions. Crushed rock fill should be tamped into the space behind the wall. The top foot can be filled with top soil.

Thomas Church, Design; F. W. Bryant, Jr., Photo

Retaining wall curved like a dam against thrust of hillside. Note how tree was saved by protective wall to shield roots

Leonard Delano, Photo

Reinforced concrete wall, holding steep bank, requires additional protection of soil-holding plants on slope above it

John Robinson, Photo

Split redwood logs used to hold back slope, rest on arms thrust into hill; plantings retard runoff, conceal the logs

V-groove redwood siding on face of 4-foot retaining wall conceals the massive substructure built of old railroad ties

Hillside held in check by series of retaining walls built of used railroad ties, which are also set alongside brick steps

Low tree wall holds soil around roots after grading lowered garden level; cut grapestakes, driven short way into ground

A line of drain tile should be placed in back of the wall along the bottom. Tiles should be set loosely, their open joints covered with tar paper, and sloped to a drop of 1 inch in 100 feet. The line should drain into a sump or storm drain that will not be under water during heavy rainfall.

TREE WALLS

Sometimes in the grading of a new homesite, the lay of the land around a tree is disturbed, and the tree will either be left in an island of dirt higher than the new grade or in a hole that is lower.

Tree Wells: When the ground level is to be raised, a wall should be built around the tree before grading is done so the soil can be piled up against it. The wall then becomes a well. The simplest wall will suf-

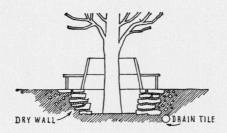

DRY WALL   DRAIN TILE

fice, as there is no great amount of soil to be held back. Use brick, dry-set stone, sidewalk chunks. Place drain tile on the upside to keep the tree well from becoming a sump during winter. Build plank benches around the top of the well to conceal it and make it safe.

Tree Walls: When the grade is lowered, large trees cannot be replanted, and yet their roots must be kept covered with soil. The reverse of the well—a raised bed—should be built to retain the soil. Since it will

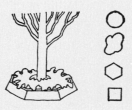

become a prominent feature in the garden, the raised bed should be carefully designed. The wall does not have to be overly strong, for its retaining function is minor, but it should be reasonably watertight so it won't allow water to sluice away from the tree roots. The wall can be cast in concrete or built of mortared brick or stone. Redwood stakes can also be used, driven into the ground around the tree, providing care is taken to avoid damaging the tree roots.

Edward Huntsman-Trout, Design; Aplin-Dudley Studios, Photo

WALKS · PATIO FLOORS

DOWN TO BEDROCK . . . what comes first?

CHECKLIST FOR HOME PAVING

Truth is that probably no one type of paving will meet your specifications 100 percent. Each has its strong and weak points which you will want to assess.

The chapters that follow discuss each surfacing material in detail, describe its advantages and shortcomings and tell how to put it in place. As you read over this information, keep in mind this set of questions:

1. *Surface texture:* Is the paving too rough for small children, too slick for old people? Is it smooth enough for dancing, rugged enough for action games? Will it soak up food stains around the barbecue? Can you slide furniture around on it easily?

2. *Appearance:* Will the color, pattern, or texture blend with your house design and garden plan? Does it have to match indoor flooring? Will it glare in the summer sun, or will it be on a shady side that needs reflected light? Do you want paving that is, or seems to be, soft under foot? Will it combine with other surfacings?

3. *Maintenance:* How easy will it be to clean? Does it collect dirt and dust? Can you remove lawn cuttings and leaves readily? Easy to sweep or wash, or must it be scrubbed clean? Will weeds grow through it? Does it require constant raking or rolling? Does it track into the house? Can food stains be removed from it?

4. *Durability:* Do you want long-lasting or temporary paving? Would you be willing to work it over each spring? How much of a job will this be? What is most likely to go wrong with it? What will frost, snow, rainwater, or excessive heat do to it?

5. *Cost:* Is the material expensive or moderate in cost? Can you save labor cost by doing all or part of the work? Any "sleepers" in the cost picture—e. g., drainage provisions, unstable soil, special processes? Are the materials obtainable in your locality or must they be imported at high freight cost?

6. *Application:* If you want to put it down yourself, is it a material that you can handle? Will you have to rent or buy special equipment? Can the materials be delivered to the point of application? How long does the job take, one week-end or six? Is it a one-man or two-man job? How soon can it be used? Is this the season to install it?

ADVANCE PREPARATIONS

No matter which type of paving you select, its lifespan will be affected by the foundation you provide for it. On stable, well-drained soils, you can sometimes dispense with sub-base. But if your soil or climate is unfriendly, you will need to protect the paving with a rock or gravel pad that will shield it from soil heaving due to the moisture locked in the ground. Often, the rock pad alone will keep the water from collecting directly under the paving, but sometimes additional provisions are necessary to carry it off.

Drainage: Excess water that collects beneath paving may be drawn off by drain tiles installed under the center or around the edge of the paved area.

Place drain tiles in a narrow trench about 12 inches deep. Lay tiles (3- or 4-inch dia.) in bottom of trench end-to-end. Wrap joints loosely with tar paper to keep silt from filling them. Pack gravel around the tile to a depth of 6 inches, then replace soil above it. Soak the fill thoroughly, preferably for several days, before laying any paving over it.

Run the line of tile (1" drop per 100') to a natural drainage point, such as a storm sewer or street drain. If this is impossible, you can often dispose of the water by digging a sump with a post hole auger. Dig down 6 or 8 feet to sandy soil, fill with rocks and gravel. Encase top foot with a section of 8-inch drain tile.

For an elaborate system, you can lay branching lines of tile that empty into a central line of bell tile that carries the water to an outfall. Systems of this complexity are probably best planned by a professional.

Grading: Once you're satisfied with the drainage, you can grade the site to the right depth for the particular paving, as recommended in the chapters that follow.

If you have to dig out soil, disturb as little as possible. If you dig too deep, tamp in fill, soak it, and tamp again after it settles. Filled areas take many months to duplicate the firm texture of native soil.

To determine how deep the area needs to be dug out, use a line-level to locate high and low points and establish grade.

First, stake off the area in squares, say 5 or 10 feet on a side. Next, determine the grade for the surface of the finished paving and mark this point on a stake with a saw cut (chalk marks rub off). Attach a chalk line at the cut and stretch it down a row of stakes. Hang the line-level in its center, and draw the line taut. Level the string and mark the point where it touches each stake with a saw cut. Repeat with other rows of stakes until all are notched at grade. You now can find out how far down to dig: on each stake, measure down the thickness of the paving plus its subgrade plus an allowance for pitch of 1 inch in 10 feet.

Douglas Baylis, Design; Philip Fein, Photo

Sometimes looked down upon as "economy" surfacing, gravel is dressy enough to fit into a sophisticated garden setting

LOOSE AGGREGATES . . . quick, inexpensive — smart

Many homeowners have need for inexpensive, easily-applied surfacing materials to supplement existing paving or to put down temporarily.

The low-cost surfacing may be needed for paving secondary areas, such as paths, service yard, or floor of the potting shed; it may serve as a stopgap, to make a muddy area navigable through a winter or to rough-in a patio while the budget is convalescing from the shock of buying the house.

For these purposes, there are several suitable and practical forms of surfacing obtainable. Some of them, though low in cost, are attractive and dressy, well worth renewing when they wear out.

TANBARK

Tanbark is a by-product of the leather-making industry. It consists of oak bark chips that have been used in tanning leather.

Not always easy to obtain, it is usually available only in areas where a tannery is located. It may be bought at the tannery cash-and-carry or from nurseries in the locality.

Tanbark makes an attractive carpeting for certain garden areas. It *can* be put down for a patio, but it is too easily scattered to be satisfactory in a large area. Confined between headers, it makes an attractive path, soft and springy under foot. Spread generously in the children's play yard, under the swings and slide, it cushions a falling child from injury.

It is not affected by weather. Moisture does it no harm; and it can be walked on when saturated. It has double value to the gardener, for when it is worn out as a paving, it can be added to the compost pile or worked into the soil.

Tanbark is put down on top of the soil for a pathway. In a boxed play yard, it should be placed over 2 or 3 inches of gravel and sand for drainage.

Amount Needed: For 100 square feet of 3-inch surfacing, you would need about 1 cubic yard. A ton covers 175 square feet.

Charles Prentice, Photo

Philip Fein, Photo

Philip Fein, Photo

Ron Partridge, Photo

GRAVEL SYMPOSIUM. Upper left: Path of flagstones carries the walker across gravel terrace. **Upper right:** A barbecue terrace completely surfaced with gravel, held in place by used railroad-tie headers. **Lower left:** Weatherbeaten railroad ties used for steps, filled with gravel. **Lower right:** This mowing strip of concrete bricks keeps gravel from the lawn

GRAVEL

Gravel or crushed rock will provide a clean and fairly durable surface for paths and service areas. Some homeowners have successfully used it for a temporary patio.

It stands up best, of course, when put down as a topping over a more permanent bed of redrock or decomposed granite. But it will give several season's service put right on the ground.

Gravel has certain weaknesses. It is a slow and uncomfortable surface to walk on; the little stones work their way into women's sandals and open-toed shoes; it gradually vanishes into the soil beneath and it must be refreshened from time to time; weeds grow through it easily, and if they are not pulled out when they are small, their clinging roots will make an unsightly hole in the gravel when they are yanked out when full grown; and if placed next to a lawn, the stones get kicked into the grass where they knick the blades of a lawnmower.

Pointers: Gravel is sold in a range of sizes. Don't buy too fine or too coarse a grade. Most practical size is around ½ inch. The smaller pea gravel sticks to shoes and is constantly tracked into the house. The largest sizes are hard to walk on. Don't buy mixed sizes: the small stones quickly work their way down and leave only the big ones on the surface.

Lay gravel about 1½ to 2 inches thick. If put down in a thinner layer, it is soon kicked aside and the soil beneath comes to the surface. If put down too thickly, it makes too flexible a footing.

For best results, it should be rolled. Rake it over the area in thin layers, dampen it, and roll it down. Repeat until the area is built up to the final thickness. You will have to rake and re-roll it from time to time thereafter.

Place gravel beds between headers of wood, bricks, or concrete. Keep it away from the house. A shaggy doormat or a strip of lawn between the doorway and the gravel paving will help keep it out of the house.

Amount Needed: For 100 square feet of 1-inch surfacing, you will require ½ cubic yard.

REDROCK

Redrock is a form of rocky clay soil that compacts solidly when dampened and rolled.

It is used in volume in foundation work, where it is put down as a cushion to protect concrete from soil movement. In garden paving, it can either be laid by itself or as a pad for a dressier topping.

When put down alone, redrock provides a surface that is clean and hard, and if of good quality, it will not turn to mud in the rain. The surface wears away, however, and breaks down into dust. When its surface is no longer satisfactory as a paving material, it can be covered with a topping of a more durable substance.

The secret of achieving a satisfactory redrock paving is in putting it down in 1-inch layers and rolling each layer thoroughly. Dampen each layer before rolling. A 3-inch depth is sufficient.

Amount Needed: For 100 square feet, 3 inches deep, you will need about 1 cubic yard.

DECOMPOSED GRANITE

Decomposed granite is similar to redrock but superior to it in wearing quality. If properly compacted, it forms a dense paving that is not prone to dust-off and that doesn't turn to mud when wet. It costs about a third more than redrock.

Decomposed granite is water-compacted in the same manner as redrock.

CRUSHED BRICK

Crushed brick is not strictly a "budget" paving material. In bulk it costs ten times as much as redrock, for instance, but if applied lightly over stable soil or a redrock base, it can be put down for moderate cost.

It is not designed for heavy traffic (it is actually a roofing material). Unlike gravel or crushed rock, the fragments break up and wear down. But it brings to the garden a fresh and lively color, which if used in moderation, gives striking accent to plantings. The venetian red is too intense to be spread over broad areas—a driveway covered with it is almost blinding.

Obtainable through building material dealers and roofing contractors.

Amount Needed: For 100 square feet of 1-inch topping, order 6 sacks.

Scott Imlay, Design; Philip Fein, Photo

Tanbark flooring for garden work center. Soft under foot, can later be turned into the soil. Adobe block steps and wall

Osmundson & Staley, Design; John Robinson, Photo

Steps and pathway are surfaced with water-compacted red rock, packed within redwood 2x8's. Wall is dry-stone type

SOIL-CEMENT . . . good if the soil is amenable

Have you ever wondered what would happen if you tried to surface a driveway or path by simply mixing Portland cement with your garden soil?

If your soil is the right type to respond to this treatment, it should surprise you by producing a hard, dry surface that will require negligible upkeep.

The surface is suitable for pathways, patios, driveways, and parking places. Not as strong as concrete, it is not adequate for areas that are subjected to heavy traffic or substantial soil movement.

TEST YOUR SOIL

Not every type of soil will respond to treatment with cement. Heavy clay and adobe soils usually will not respond, but loamy or sandy soils usually can be hardened satisfactorily. Soil must be reasonably free from decayed vegetable matter, trash; sod or grass must be removed.

If you have any doubts about your soil and how it will work as concrete, you can run an experiment as follows:

1. Make two small wooden forms 4 inches deep and 6 inches square.

2. Dig up an area 1 foot square and 4 inches deep in the location where you plan to apply the cement.

3. Pulverize the soil and mix in 4 pounds of cement.

4. Work in enough water so a small sample of the mixture will retain the finger prints when squeezed in the hand, but will not noticeably wet the fingers, and will not release excess water. Too much or too little water will cause poor results. The mixture should not be muddy or wet when packed.

5. Shovel the mixture into the two boxes and tamp each box full with an iron-faced tamper so the mixture is compacted as hard as possible.

6. Cover boxes with damp earth and let one sample harden for a couple of days and the other for a week.

7. After samples have hardened, remove from box, place one in a bucket of water for 2 hours, and then place in the sun for 2 hours. Repeat this 3 times a day for a day or two. The samples should not soften or break down. This is particularly true of the sample left in the box for a week. If the samples soften, try soil from another location or try using more cement.

HOW TO MIX IT INTO THE SOIL

If your soil passes the tests, you are ready to proceed.

First break up the soil in the area to a depth of six inches. You can do this with a spade, hoe, and rake; or, more comfortably, with garden tractor or rotary tiller (you can rent a rotary tiller in many localities).

No dirt or clay clods should be left. Rake out the larger rocks. Figure on a soil and cement mixture of 9 parts soil to 1 part dry cement, based on cubic measurements. (Example: a 6-inch driveway 40 feet long and 9 feet wide would contain 180 cubic feet of soil and would require 20 sacks of cement.)

Dump the cement in little piles, evenly distributed over the prepared surface, and rake it out into a thin layer. Work it into the soil with a hoe, or churn the whole mix with a rotary tiller. Even out the surface with a rake.

Tamp the surface with a heavy block on a handle, or the edge of a heavy plank. This will disclose low spots left by tilling and raking, which should be filled with soil and cement mixture and again tamped until smooth.

Sprinkle the surface with a fine spray from the garden hose. Don't let the water puddle. The dry cement pulls the water down like moisture soaking into a blotter. Continue this fine spray sprinkling as long as the water is readily soaked up.

As soon as the surface has dried so that a lawn roller won't pick up mud, go over it with the roller. Use a 350-pound roller. You can rent one for a moderate fee.

When the area has been compacted enough so that footprints don't show, sprinkle it again with a fine spray until it is pretty well soaked. However, don't wet it so much that it turns to mud. Frequent light sprinklings should be continued daily for 4 or 5 days.

Soil-cement dries more slowly than ordinary concrete, but it should be kept damp as long as it will absorb water. In dry climates, you can protect the surface and lengthen the drying period by topping the area temporarily with an inch or so of loose soil.

The final, cured surface will not look much different from the soil you started with; but it will be clean, free from dust, and weatherproof. It may show a few small cracks, but they are harmless.

FORMS AND EDGING

It would be wise to use forms around the perimeter of the area, and to build a retaining edge of brick or wood. Otherwise, the mixture is likely to crumble at the edges. This is particularly important in the case of pathways and other narrow strips of paving.

If you can't finish the whole project in one day or wish to add to it later, bury a 2 by 6-inch board, surface high, at the uncompleted end. This will give you a sharp edge from which to continue.

Charles R. Pearson, Photos

1. Rotary tiller, set for 6-inch depth, pulverizes soil. Rocks, clods go out later

2. Portland cement dumped in evenly spaced piles, 1 sack to 18 square feet

3. Dry cement is raked from each pile by hand until spread in thin, even layer

4. Several passes by rotary tiller, doing same work as a flour sifter, mixes the loose soil and cement to full depth

5. Edge of long, heavy board is used to tamp soil and compact it. Low spots filled with soil-cement mix before wetting

6. Water sprayed on in mist to avoid puddling, permit the cement in compacted areas to absorb moisture quickly, evenly

7. Rolling is repeated until surface is footprint-proof. The appearance is smoother after repeated spraying over week

Cliff May, Design; Maynard Parker, Photo

Asphalt paving used in secondary patio off the master bedroom. Paving was professionally laid at the time house was built

ASPHALT . . . most for the money

Recommend asphalt paving to a man for his patio, and you will probably stir him to an uncomfortable vision. He will see a picture of himself on a hot day slowly vanishing along with his furniture into the sticky pavement, like the unfortunate captives of the La Brea Tar Pits.

Some years ago, when asphalt paving wasn't greatly different from roofing tar, this picture would have had a measure of truth in it. But today, thanks to years of research by the asphalt industry, some varieties of blacktop can be entrusted with important services in the garden.

Blacktop has long been accepted for paving driveways, paths, and service yards; but it is also used effectively by some designers for patio and terrace surfacing. Some use it in combination with other materials, using brick or concrete for the dining and sitting areas, and spreading the asphalt far and wide for an extension of the patio. Since it costs less per square foot than either brick or concrete, even when it is laid by a contractor, it can be used to give the homeowner a much larger paved area for his money.

PRO AND CON

Blacktop does have some shortcomings — but it has compensating virtues as well.

If not properly mixed with the right amount of asphalt and if inadequately compacted, it will soften in warm weather and will show the footprints of sharp-toed chairs and tables, the tracks of skates or iron-wheeled garden carts. Properly installed over a solid, interlocked pad of rocks, it should have almost as tough a surface as brick or concrete.

On hot days, asphalt paving becomes scorching, because the black surface soaks up the sun's energy, and it retains the heat long after the sun has set. However, it doesn't bounce it into the house as reflected heat. Like concrete or bricks, blacktop can be cooled to a comfortable barefoot temperature by dousing it with water.

Asphalt pavement demands less material than concrete. A ½ or ¾-inch topping on a good gravel or stone base will usually serve for driveways and 1½ to 2 inches for sidewalks or patios. The asphalt will crack, bulge, or sag if the soil shifts underneath it, but the damage is easily patched—unlike concrete that simply gives way under stress and leaves the homeowner with a difficult repair job on his hands.

Blacktop is quickly put down and is ready to walk on in a couple of hours (but hold back the chairs for a week). A 500-square-foot area can easily be placed in a morning. Although the paving job calls for special equipment, the monstrous machines that you meet on vacation detours are not needed for garden paving. In fact, under some conditions you can put it down yourself with a heavy roller and a hand pouring pot.

Asphalt paving requires some maintenance. Weeds and plants grow right through it unless the soil has been previously sterilized. The watertight asphalt freakishly duplicates hothouse conditions in the soil beneath it and accelerates seed germination. This can be prevented by doctoring the soil with a sterilant such as common rock salt, or commercial products such as arsenic trioxide, polybor chlorate (if you can get it), or borascule. Avoid using diesel oil or crankcase drainings for they will prevent the asphalt from curing. If carefully applied, the sterilants will not injure plantings alongside the treated area unless their roots reach into the sterilized zone.

KINDS OF ASPHALT PAVING

Asphalt is a semi-liquid that solidifies on exposure to the air. When used in paving, its simple function is to bind and seal a rock pad into a solid waterproof mass. It is applied in various ways, either hot or cold.

The most refined and durable of the various asphaltic mixtures—and, as such, also the most expensive—is known as "hot-mixed, hot-applied asphaltic concrete." This paving is formed by coating crushed rock with a penetration form of asphalt cement. When these are first put down together, the asphalt is in a liquid state, due to heat applied at the manufacturing plant. As it cools, it solidifies and binds together the aggregates.

Another type of pavement is known as "cold-mix." This mixture is made by combining graded aggregates with either of two types of liquid asphalt. One, known as "cut-back asphalt," is a variety that relies on volatile naphthas to hold the asphalt in solution. When the mixture has been put down as paving, the naphthas quickly evaporate and leave the asphalt cement to hold the aggregates together.

The other type of cold-mix is made with an asphaltic emulsion which relies on a water-soap solution to hold the asphalt in suspension. Like the cut-backs, the emulsifying agents evaporate and leave behind the asphalt cement.

The rapidity with which the carrier—e. g., the naphtha or the water-soap solution — evaporates is controlled by the type and proportion of the carrier used in the mixture. There are 5 types of emulsion and 16 cut-backs obtainable, graded according to their setting speed into slow, medium, and fast curing.

Larry Halprin, Design; Philip Fein, Photo

Homeowner wanted lots of paving put down cold plant-mix himself. Hauled the mix from asphalt plant in his trailer, put it down, and rolled and rerolled it with a rented power pavement roller

APPLYING ASPHALT

The home handyman who is bold enough to attempt it can put down asphalt paving successfully if he doesn't try to take on too ambitious a project. But for many reasons the paving of a large area like a patio, terrace, or even a service yard is best entrusted to a contractor.

The paving contractor has special equipment for compacting the rock fill and spraying on the liquefied asphalt or applying hot-mix. He can give you the smooth, level surface without "bird baths" that is hard for the amateur to achieve with limited equipment and lack of know-how. Furthermore, his charges are likely to be reasonable enough, even including the rough grading and installation of header boards.

If you decide to have a contractor do the work, you would be wise to protect him and yourself by following written specifications for the job. You can secure recommended specifications by writing to the nearest office of the Asphalt Institute. Provide them with full details: kind of soil to be paved (adobe, sandy, loam, free-draining, etc.) nearness of your home to an asphalt mixing plant, drainage conditions, square footage of area to be covered, and purposes to which it will be put, whether patio, terrace, service yard, driveway, or path.

If you would like to try to pave with asphalt yourself, you would be wise to start off with a modest project, such as a path or a short driveway. Following are various methods that the amateur can try.

COLD PLANT-MIX

For some purposes, the home handyman may find cold plant-mix well worth attempting (the hot-mix is strictly for pros). In small areas like a path, where it can be hand-tamped, or in an area subject to vehicular compaction, such as a driveway, the amateur can cope with it successfully. But for large areas, such as a patio, terrace, or large service yard, he would probably find himself in trouble, unless he could rent a gasoline-driven tamper or a small power roller.

Main objection to cold plant-mix is its slow curing time. Furniture will indent it for 6 months or more. One way this handicap has been overcome is to lay the paving just before the winter closes in. The surface can be walked on during the rainy months, and if properly applied it will sustain furniture when patio weather returns in the spring.

You can only use this mixture if you live close enough to a mixing plant to pick it up and if you have a light truck or trailer for hauling it. Most asphalt mixing plants are geared to the volume needs of paving contractors, and they are reluctant to deliver small quantities, such as you would require for garden paving, but they are usually willing to sell it on a come-and-get-it basis.

Schedule of Operations: If you decide to use this mix, here are the steps you would probably follow:

1. Level the ground and scrape it away to firm soil. Apply soil sterilant to keep weeds from growing through.

2. Install permanent headers around rim of area to be surfaced, because asphalt paving tends to crumble at the edge.

3. Put down a 4-inch layer of crushed stone, 1 to 1½ inch in size. Level and roll with a heavy roller or compact with a power vibrator.

Cliff May, Design; W. P. Woodcock, Photo

Asphalt-paved entryway provides a subdued, non-glare surface in contrast with the white of painted brick walls of Spanish-style home

4. Put down a second layer of small crushed stone, ½ to ¾ inch in size. These are the key rocks that lock the large stones in place, increase density, and provide a smooth top surface. Work them down into the voids between the larger rocks. Wet down thoroughly for compaction. *Let dry to damp condition.*

5. Shovel emulsion-type cold-mix on the damp rock, rake it out evenly with a garden rake to a depth of 1 inch. (If cut-back cold-mix is used, the stone or gravel base must be *dry* and made tacky by priming with a light coat of liquid asphalt.

6. Roll it. Wait 2 hours, and roll again.

7. For a smooth surface, scatter sand or pea gravel over surface and roll again.

Materials Needed: For 100 square feet of 1-inch surfacing laid over a 4-inch rock or gravel base, you will need about:

Cold-mix, emulsion or cut-back... ½ ton
Crushed rock (1½″ to 1″).......1½ tons
Key rock (¾″ to ¼″)........... ½ ton
or
Sandy-binder graded gravel......2 tons

EMULSION BONDED

Another method of laying blacktop is to put down a pad of graded rock, coat the surface with rapid-setting emulsified asphalt, and cover with sand.

This can readily be done by the garden handyman, and the resulting surface is likely to be more immediately usable than one produced by cold-mix because the emulsions available for this purpose set up more rapidly.

The asphaltic emulsion can be obtained in bulk from asphalt storage lots located in many cities and rural areas.

How to Apply: The simplest way to apply it to a small area is to pour it from a garden sprinkling can. Be sure to clean out the sprinkler with water immediately after each application. If you allow traces of emulsion to remain in the can, you will have to remove them with kerosene.

Another easy way is to pour it from a square 5-gallon can, cut as shown in the drawing. Hold the

handle in the left hand, place the right hand under the bottom, and tip the can to produce on even flow from the pouring lip. Walk slowly backwards, pouring as you go. Recommendation: Practice with water until you perfect your technique before pouring the emulsion.

Larry Halprin, Design; Philip Fein, Photo

Owner-applied asphalt paving for patio surfacing. Put down in late fall, furniture kept off for several months to allow curing. (Continuation of garden shown on page 45)

The very best way to apply it is to rent a portable spray outfit. This is a two-man rig that is available in the few localities where asphalt is manufactured. The pump is designed to attach to the standard 50-gallon drum. Your neighbor works the pump while you manipulate a spray nozzle on the end of a short boom.

Sequence of Operations: Preparation of the rock pad is the same as outlined above under cold-mix. After the rock is down and rolled, proceed as follows:

1. Spray or pour emulsion on the rock at a rate of 1½ gallons per square yard.

2. Let cure for 24 hours, then pour on a lighter application of the emulsion (¼ gal. per sq. yd.) and with a broom, brush onto the surface a coating of coarse sand or light pea gravel, 25 to 30 pounds per square yard. Roll immediately and *thoroughly.*

3. Let cure 24 hours, and if surface is not smooth enough to suit you, repeat the sand treatment.

4. Let cure 24 hours. It is then ready for use—unless you think another sand coat is needed. It is a good idea to let a surplus of sand remain on the surface for a while to absorb or "set" any excess of asphalt.

The secret of succeeding with this pavement is to roll it over and over again during the curing period.

Caution: Do not attempt to work with asphalt emulsions during rainy weather. A shower on freshly poured emulsion will ruin it.

Materials Needed: To put down 100 square feet of paving on 4 inches of crushed stone, with 3 applications of sand surfacing:

Crushed stone .... 1½ tons
Key stones .... ½ ton
Asphalt emulsion, rapid setting..25 gals.
Sand or pea gravel—
   one application ....300 pounds
   three applications ....800 pounds

PATENTED PAVING

In some localities, a patented blend of asphalt emulsion and light aggregates may be purchased in cartons or drums. You simply pour a measured amount of water into the container, empty the mix on the rock pad, and trowel it out with a mason's float to ½ or 1-inch depth. The product is designed to be used as-is on paths and service yards, but needs the addition of Portland cement when used for patio surfacing. It may be put down directly on stable soil, but a rock pad is essential on heavy clay or other tricky soils.

COLORING ASPHALT

Asphalt paving may be attractively colored with plastic paints specially manufactured for the purpose. The paints have stood up successfully on roller rinks and outdoor dance floors. The colors are soft in tone, range from light tan to dark green.

Eckbo, Royston & Williams, Design; Ernest Braun, Photo

Part of garden where asphalt paving substitutes for lawn, other ground cover. Asphalt topping exposes rocks for texture

Tommy Tomson, Design; William C. Aplin, Photo

Basket weave pattern formed with mixture of new and used bricks, gives both pattern and texture to this spacious terrace

BRICKS . . . a pleasing surface for any garden

One of the most rewarding jobs on the home-owner's list of projects is paving with brick. It's difficult to make serious mistakes with bricks if the simpler methods are followed. If, in paving a path or terrace with brick in sand, the job turns out wavy and grass grows between the bricks, the home-owner can claim a desire for informal, naturalistic effects. If the first attempt is not pleasing, a complete renovation calls for only his own labor.

PRO AND CON

Bricks give warm color to the garden and add a pleasant contrast in texture. Because they are small units, they set up a scale against which the eye measures the rest of the garden, a scale which doesn't dwarf even a pansy.

Bricks are easily set in place—in fact, brick-in-sand pavement is probably the simplest to install of any garden paving. However, let no man persuade you that a brick patio can be laid in a day. Grading and screeding are time-consuming operations, and the fitting of bricks in place may take several week ends. In fact, after you have laid a 3,000-brick patio,

you may never want to see another brick again. The secret of getting the job done painlessly is to take it on in manageable sections and not to attempt too much at one time.

Under most conditions, bricks produce a solid and durable paving surface. If laid on sand, however, they often come through the winter with a deck roll that has to be ironed out each spring by taking up and resetting patches of brickwork. Some of the softer types tend to disintegrate in winter under a rain-freeze-thaw cycle.

The rough surface of the varieties of brick usually used for garden paving reduces glare and gives good traction, but it makes a sluggish surface for dancing and games.

Bricks are difficult to keep clean—their open pores readily absorb oil, grease, paint, ground-in adobe; the joints accumulate dust and dirt, dimes and breadcrumbs. Weeds and crab grass work their way between them. However, the porosity that makes bricks difficult to clean also makes them good for air cooling. They readily soak up water, and as it evaporates it cools the air, makes the bricks cool under foot.

(49)

Jerry Anson, Photo

Bricks on sand, laid in running bond; immaculate craftsmanship evident in careful fitting of brick ring around base of tree

Philip Fein, Photo

Bricks on sand laid in variation of jack-on-jack pattern; border course set in mortar to retain sand-bedded bricks

Philip Fein, Photo

Informal paving for recreation terrace achieved by laying used bricks in basket weave pattern with irregular joints

KINDS OF BRICK

Visit a local building materials dealer to see the full range of size, texture, and color—red, orange, yellow, brown, gray, blue-black—you may choose from.

Of the bewildering variety of bricks turned out by the brickyards, only two classes are favored for garden surfacing: slick-surfaced *face* brick and rough-textured *common* brick. Face brick is less frequently laid than common because it is much more expensive and its smooth surface calls for matching mortar joints, carefully struck with professional style. Face bricks include roman brick and paving brick.

The more popular common brick is obtainable in three choices:

1. *Wire-cut brick* is square-cut, but the texture is rougher, with little pit marks on the faces. Lay it to expose the edge if you want a smoother surface.

2. *Sand-mold brick* is smooth-textured, easy to clean, and is slightly larger on one face than the other because it must be turned out of a mold.

3. *Clinker brick* has been overburned, which gives it black patches and irregularities on the surface. Use it alone, or in combinations, for a rough, cobblestone effect.

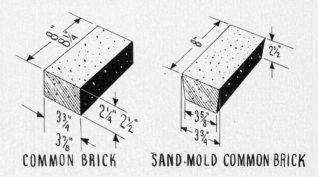

COMMON BRICK   SAND-MOLD COMMON BRICK

Try to buy common brick that is hard-burned, for it will outlast "green" brick. When well-burned, it is usually dark red; under-burned runs to a salmon color. Give it a "ring test" by striking it with a hammer. Well-burned brick gives a clear, high-pitched, metallic sound; under-done brick, a dull thud, like a block of wood.

But don't scorn the softer brick. In a paving as it wears unevenly, it acquires a comfortable, weathered look.

Used bricks, with their uneven surface and streaks of old mortar, make an attractive informal pavement. They can often be bought in their raw state for less than new bricks; but cleaning them is a time-consuming chore, especially if the old mortar is tougher than the bricks themselves. If you buy them already cleaned, you are likely to pay more than for new brick, because of the labor involved in sprucing them up for sale.

Caution: Ascertain if your dealer has sufficient bricks of the variety you need to see you through your project. There is usually enough dimensional variation between bricks, even those from the same kiln, to complicate your work if you are fitting them closely together; and if you have to complete the job with a different variety or some from another brick works, you may find it impossible to complete the lineal or color pattern that you have started.

PAVING PATTERNS

You can invent new brick paving patterns. Cut out some cardboard bricks and try it sometime. But the pattern you put into your paving shouldn't be so "busy" that you will tire of it. If in doubt, use one well tested by time.

Here are three of the perennially popular, unobtrusive patterns with one suggested variation for each.

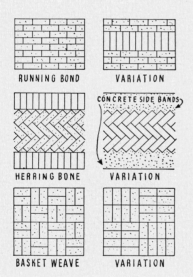

RUNNING BOND   VARIATION

CONCRETE SIDE BANDS

HERRING BONE   VARIATION

BASKET WEAVE   VARIATION

Note that your choice of pattern will be affected by whether or not you lay the bricks with open or closed joints. The dimensional variations common to clay brick make some patterns difficult to realize when the bricks are butted tightly against each other. A pattern like jack-on-jack, for instance, is hard to follow through a large area. Basket weave when laid solid will produce a curious effect: a ½-inch hole turns up in the center of each block of 8 bricks. Least troublesome pattern for solid joints is running bond.

When space is left open between bricks, on the other hand, the variations in brick dimensions can easily be taken up by widening or reducing the width of the joints.

Thornton Ladd, Design; William C. Aplin, Photo

Copper strip separates the bricks from the concrete on this terrace. Bricks laid jack-on-jack over slab, mortared in place

Scott-Imlay, Design; Philip Fein, Photo

Irregular bricks, laid on sand with redwood header boards; contrast in color, texture with tree mulch of smooth pebbles

Charles R. Pearson, Photo

Bricks laid in herringbone pattern have well-groomed appearance; give the impression of smooth, finished workmanship

Jerry A. Anson, Photo

Mellow warmth of the brick paving adds to the restful charm of this patio. Bricks on sand, laid in herringbone variation

Eckbo, Royston & Williams, Design; Childress & Halberstadt, Photo

Concrete and bricks in combination. Section left open for child's sand box; can be filled in when child outgrows it

Maynard Parker, Photo

Division between sheltered and exposed terrace marked by two colors of bricks, different treatment of mortar joints

When paving a large area with closed joints, you can break up the monotony of the surface by changing the direction of the bond within the paving pattern or by fitting the bricks into a redwood or cedar grid system, as shown below:

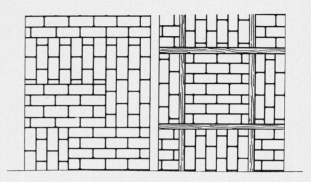

Cutting Bricks: Few brick patios can be laid without some bricks having to be cut. *Save your cutting* of bricks to the last so that you can do them all at one time. It is a "squat," not a "stoop," operation. A brick-layer becomes skillful at cutting soft brick by giving it a sharp rap with a sturdy trowel. He uses a *cold chisel* or *brick hammer* for trimming and for making irregular cuts. You probably will do best with the *brick set.* The bricklayer holds it in place and gives it one hard knock with a heavy hammer. You may get better results by tapping it lightly to cut a groove across one or more sides before giving the final severing blow. Either way, have the brick on a solid level base. Hold the brick set as shown

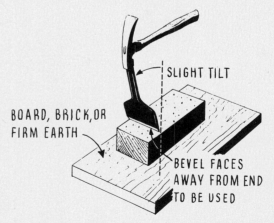

SLIGHT TILT

BOARD, BRICK, OR FIRM EARTH

BEVEL FACES AWAY FROM END TO BE USED

below. Keep it sharpened. Smooth up uneven cuts with an abrasive stone, or if the brick is soft by rubbing it with another brick.

LAYING BRICKS IN SAND

Laying bricks in sand is a simple job for the amateur. But the finishing touches call for good workmanship and skill. Just grade your soil, put on

BRICKS IN SAND. 1. Lay brick paving with slight slant. Set headers on proper slope so sand bed can be screeded correctly

2. Smooth out sand with screed. "Ears" nailed to end of screed hold edge at proper depth, enables straight-edge to be shifted

3. Save broken bricks to be cut to fill in half sizes needed to fill pattern. Cut with brick set, mason's hammer; not hatchet

4. Make sure brick is firmly bedded by striking it with hammer handle; if too high or low, remove, adjust sand, reset

5. Go over entire surface with iron tamp or heavy post; or place 2x4 across several bricks and pound with maul

6. After bricks are set in place, shovel sand onto surface, then sweep into cracks; cement can be added, if sand is dry

Victor Wandmayer, Design; Philip Fein, Photo

Bricks used in terrace of brick house are laid without mortar to provide contrast to the texture and color of the walls

Frederick Confer, Clarence Tantau, Jr., Design; Ron Partridge, Photo

Redwood headers divide brickwork into grid pattern; bricks within each square laid in running bond, alternate direction

V. P. Jensen, Design; William C. Aplin, Photo

Wide brick walk with sawtooth edge for planting beds; sand-bedded bricks are laid in running bond in redwood headers

a cushion of sand, lay your bricks as close together as possible, and sweep sand or quarry dust into the cracks. You get a solid paving, with no pockets

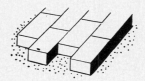

likely to catch water. It either drains across the bricks or seeps into the sand. If a brick does settle too badly out of line, just pry it up and build up its foundation with more sand.

Grading: Do some careful calculating before grading your soil and sand. Bricks in sand will settle. Better give them some clearance.

Use a 2 by 4-inch board of convenient length as a screed board for your grading. Notch the ends, or nail pieces on, depending on how deep you must go. But don't use one more than 10 or 12 feet long. If you have to span a wider area, put stakes or timbers in the middle, line up with the edges, and use them as additional guides. Place spirit level on top of board.

Pushing dirt around this way isn't easy. Loosen up the top soil a little, grade it the best you can, and tamp it well. Sand will take care of slight irregularities.

Screeding: The most crucial operation is screeding (leveling) the sand. Grade it down exactly, and

then don't step on it. Walk out on the bricks as you lay them, or put down boards if you have to step on the sand. Check levelness with spirit level.

Setting Bricks: In a walk, you can lay in bricks experimentally to see how your pattern works out for size. It may be worth while to do this before putting down the firm outside edges, just to avoid too many cut bricks. But in a large, irregular-shaped terrace, you'll just have to start laying your bricks and hope for the best. Here's one worthwhile tip: Start working from the middle of one side and lay a ribbon of your pattern all the way across the area in whatever direction you wish it to go. Then work from this middle ribbon toward each side. As you get near the edges, tighten or loosen the joints as necessary so that you can end up with whole bricks whenever possible.

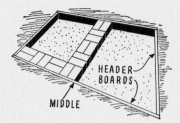

Edging: Give a firm tight edge to this kind of paving, for appearance and for permanent stability. Do this first and make the whole job easier.

One common way is to make a complete border of brick laid up with mortar joints (see description of technique below) on a thin bed of mortar or concrete.

Lay them flat, on edge, or on end, depending on how strong you want the border.

Another way is to make your outside strip of concrete. (Standard mix: 1 part Portland cement, 2¾ parts sand, 4 parts aggregate ½ to 1½-inch screen.)

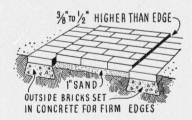

In any combination of concrete and brick, pour the concrete in forms first, then lay the brick, to get a good, sharply-defined line between the two.

A third possibility is wooden header strips, 2 by 4 inches or 2 by 6 inches, which should be firmly held in place by stakes or other reinforcement. The wood headers make the best guides for leveling up the rest of the job. When you use brick or concrete edgings as guides, you may wish to lay thin boards over them to correct their unevenness.

Any one of these can also be used throughout the paving as separators for grid patterns. But leave the exact dimensions of your grid flexible until you have laid bricks in one sample section, and have dis-

Thomas Church, Designs and Photos

Three artful variations introduced into standard patterns

Further examples of variations from brick paving patterns

covered what size will require the least cutting of bricks. For permanent headers, use redwood or cedar.

Drainage: For good drainage, give your paving a pitch, a fall of at least 1 inch in 6 feet. It's better in most cases to allow a little more. You won't notice the difference because very few apparently level areas outdoors are really dead level.

Width of Joints: You can choose between two methods of setting bricks on the sand bed: they may be butted snugly together or they can be placed ½ inch apart and the space about filled with sand.

The first method usually provides a more reliable paving because the tightly wedged bricks hold each other in place. However, such a surface is often troublesome to lay because the variations in the size and shape of the bricks may force you to a lot of exasperating trying and fitting.

When bricks are set with ½-inch sand joints, they tend to work out of position as the sand settles. This can be controlled to some degree by refilling the joints from time to time. Better practice is to mix cement with sand as described below under "dry mortar."

Materials Needed: Amount of material to order will depend on your choice of the open or closed joint. For each 100 square feet of surface bedded on a 1-inch sand bed, order as follows:

	Closed Joints	½-inch Joints
Bricks	450	400
Sand	5 cu. ft.	7 cu. ft.

Weed Control: Some weeds will inevitably straggle through brick-in-sand paving. Between the bricks, pour a general contact weed killer such as arsenic trioxide or ammonium sulfamate.

DRY MORTAR

For a more stable and permanent form of paving, add Portland cement to the sand, lay the bricks exactly as you would for brick-in-sand, and when you have finished, wet the whole paving down with a fine spray.

The cement added to the sand bed keeps the foundation from fraying at the edges and stops sand from disappearing down cracks in the ground. Cement mixed into the sand that is brushed into the joints restrains the bricks from twisting and rearing up and locks them into a homogeneous mass.

It is not so easy as it sounds to get a clean job by this method. A little cement from the dry mix is likely to stick to the bricks as you sweep across. Better scrub each brick with a brush and then play the fine spray on it. But not too much water so that a gooey mixture starts overflowing the cracks and staining the bricks again.

Materials Needed: For 100 square feet of paving on a 2-inch sand bed, with ½-inch joints, you will need:

        Bricks 400
        Cement ....1 sack
        Sand ....11 cubic feet

You will also require a hose with adjustable fine spray nozzle; pieces of wood ½x4x6 for tamping mortar between joints — a piece of orange crate works fine; and a 10-inch mason's trowel or small piece of iron bent in offset curve to rake mortar smoothly between joints.

Preparing Sand Bed: Mix sand and cement together, blending 1 part cement to 6 parts sand. Grade soil, pile sand in place, and screed level as described above.

Caution: Since your sand is likely to be damp, it will begin to set the cement as soon as the two are mixed. Put the sand-cement down as soon as possible after mixing.

Laying Brick: Lay the bricks about ½ inch apart (width of thumb) in desired pattern. Level each course and even the alignment of the bricks, by use of a straight 2 by 4 of convenient length.

When bricks are in place, mix the dry mortar, using 3 parts sand to 1 part cement. Throw the mixture on with a shovel and sweep it into the crevices between the bricks.

Tamp between each brick with a thin board to compact dry mortar and prevent undue settling when water is applied. Unless dry mix is firm and even between bricks, too much water may run down, washing the cement into the ground; or uneven pockets may be formed that will weaken the bond.

Sweep excess dry mortar off bricks. Mortar is harder to remove once it gets wet.

Adding Water: Using adjustable nozzle on garden hose, reduce water to fine hard spray of small volume. Stand on a long board to prevent bricks from getting out of alignment. Hold nozzle close to, and play over, each brick, scrubbing it with a small brush at the same time to clean surface. Don't attempt project on very hot day, as brick will suck water from mortar; and don't get bricks so wet they dilute mortar.

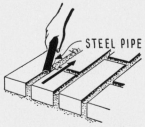

STEEL PIPE

Rake joints smooth and even with curved iron rod to give the job a finished professional look.

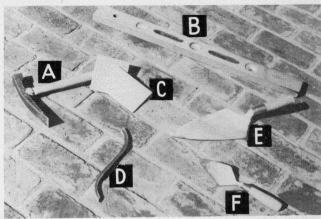

John Robinson, Photo

DRY MORTAR: 1. Paraphernalia for professional job: **a.** mason's hammer. **b.** spirit level. **c.** scraps of wood for tamping. **d.** S-shaped jointer. **e.** mason's trowel. **f.** pointing trowel

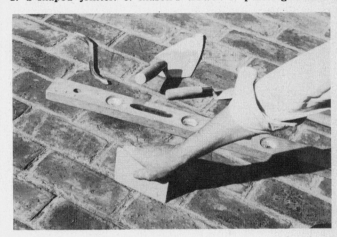

2. After sand and cement have been swept into the joints (as shown on page 53), tamp it down forcefully into the crack to be sure the mixture is solidly packed to bottom.

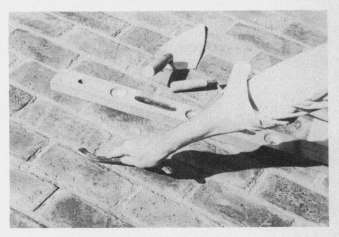

3. Wet down the bricks with fine spray or sprinkler and, after mortar has set slightly, smooth the joints with S-shaped jointer or a piece of pipe; press mortar down into the joints

Eckbo, Royston & Williams, Design; Childress & Halberstadt, Photo

Contrast of new bricks laid flat and used bricks laid on edge provides a change of pace in garden surfacing designs

Philip Fein, Photo

Novel pattern made by imbedding bricks in concrete squares for entrance walk; planting in joints is continuation of lawn

Eckbo, Royston & Williams, Design; Childress & Halberstadt, Photo

Tree well fitted into redwood gridwork separating sections of brickwork, alternating jack-on-jack and running bond

After 12 hours soak again thoroughly with heavy spray to insure penetration of moisture to full depth.

WET MORTAR

In many situations, bricks-in-sand will not be stable enough for a permanent paving. A more durable foundation is needed in localities where winters are severe or in areas that are handicapped with adobe or otherwise unstable soil that is likely to slip and settle. Best combination is to set bricks in wet mortar over a concrete slab poured on a gravel pad.

With regular patterns and tooled mortar joints, you can take full advantage of face, roman, or paving brick, to achieve a flooring that is as slick and sophisticated as tile. You can also lay common bricks on edge, jack on jack, and expose their smooth sides to gain the same effect. You can wax these varieties, if you wish.

Foundation: Lay the concrete foundation as described in the chapter on concrete paving. Put down a 4 to 6-inch pad of crushed stone and pour a 2 to 3-

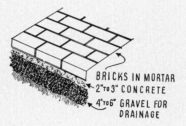

BRICKS IN MORTAR
2" to 3" CONCRETE
4" to 6" GRAVEL FOR DRAINAGE

inch slab of concrete over it. Where frost is no problem, you can decrease somewhat the depth of rock and concrete.

Setting Bricks: Laying the bricks in mortar is a job that calls for true craftsmanship—unless a deliberately "rustic" effect is desired. The mortar has to be buttered on with a brickmason's trowel, an instrument that takes patience and practice to master, and finished smooth with a pointing tool. For a description of the technique, see the chapter on building brick walls.

Materials Required: For 100 square feet of paving with ½-inch mortar joints (Type B mortar), bedded on 6-inch rock fill, you will need about:

Bricks	400
Cement	1 sack
Sand	11 cubic feet
Fireclay or lime	1 sack
Crushed stone (1½″ max.)	1½ tons

Adobe blocks laid as paving for barbecue-recreation terrace. House, outdoor fireplace, and barbecue are also built of adobe

ADOBE BLOCKS . . . yesterday's look today

Adobe bricks are doubtless at the bottom of any westerner's list of patio paving materials.

He has seen enough dissolved mission buildings and he has either heard about or struggled with the gummy, heavy clay soil called adobe so that he is entitled to a hearty mistrust of the stuff.

It may surprise him to know, then, that adobe bricks *do* make a good garden paving surface. Today's adobe block has little in common with its 18th Century predecessors, for it now carries an asphaltic stabilizer that keeps it from dissolving in winter and cracking in summer. In addition, the clay used in these bricks has nothing in common with the treacherous soil that masquerades under the name and which is the least suitable of all soils for brick-making.

Paving of adobe blocks gives a warm and friendly air to an informal patio. Their uneven shape and earthy color makes them look as though they had been down for a decade, even though laid day before yesterday. When set 1 inch apart, they provide an excellent background for a living floor of creeper and moss. They look particularly at ease in the patio of a ranch home.

Close-up of adobe blocks laid in sand, dressed with water-seal. The sand joints will soon fill in with crevice plantings

(59)

1. Adobe blocks laid on a sand bed like bricks. Space left open between the blocks will later be filled with swept sand

2. Long straight-edge used to check grade of adobe block paving. The surfacing should slope slightly for good runoff

3. Blocks may be cut with a hatchet, brick set, or the small guillotine here in use. The adobe blocks are easy to cut true

4. The thirty-pound blocks must be carefully fitted and firmly bedded. Irregularities in size makes open joints the easiest

If you live fairly near a source of supply, you will find that these large blocks cost less per square foot than brick. The standard dimensions are 8 inches wide, 16 inches long, and 4 inches thick. They weigh-in at 30 pounds apiece.

Adobe-block paving has some disadvantages. When set the inch apart that their size requires for scale, the sand joint is large enough to upset a tricycle or seize a lady's heel. Their uneven surface is too irregular for dancing, the bricks too fragile for action games. Although they do not dissolve, they wear away gradually. This produces a pleasant, weathered appearance, but it can also make the patio look unswept and dusty. In old missions and western homes, crevice planting of herbs and small flowering plants compensate for any drabness the paving might have.

LAYING ADOBE BLOCKS

Adobe blocks are laid on a sand bed in about the same manner as clay bricks. The techniques described in the chapter on laying brick paving apply equally to adobe. There are a few differences, however.

The sand bed must be solid, stable, and quite level. Adobe blocks will not bridge a hollow or straddle a hump without cracking when weight is put upon them.

Because their dimensions may vary slightly, they are usually difficult to lay in patterns that call for snug fitting. Open joints, $3/4$ to 1 inch, compensate for any irregularities.

Joints may be filled with sand or dirt or with dry mortar. The blocks are heavy enough to stay put with sand filled joints, and a dirt filling permits

Thomas Church, Design; Jon Brenneis, Photo

Adobe blocks used in paving SUNSET'S enclosed patio harmonize with western ranch house design, match scale of building

crevice planting. Adding cement to the sand (1 : 2½) keeps the joint-filling from gradually disappearing into the soil beneath, and if the joints are filled to the surface, the mortar will protect the edge of the blocks from wearing down. Asphalt stabilizer may be added to the cement-sand mixture (1½ gals. per sack of cement) as a waterseal.

Adobe blocks can be cut with a hatchet, brick set, or with a kind of small guillotine used by masons.

Surface wear can be reduced by installing adobe blocks that are richer in asphaltic stabilizer than wall blocks. They may also be dressed with masonry sealer or several coats of boiled linseed oil.

Materials Needed: For 100 square feet of adobe block paving, set with 1-inch joints, you would need:

Adobe blocks (act. size 4x7½x16)..........115
For sand bed and sand joints:
   Sand .... 7 cu. ft.
For cement mortar joints:
   Sand .... 7 cu. ft.
Portland cement .... 3 sacks
Stabilizer .... 5 gals.

You would be smart to buy a dozen extra adobes for replacements. In a large quantity of blocks, there are likely to be a few that will develop flaws or disintegrate after you put them down. You may have difficulty replacing them with blocks that match the color and texture of those previously laid unless you have extras on hand.

MAKING ADOBE BRICKS

There are several firms that specialize in making adobe blocks. They will ship them any reasonable distance, but the freight charges make the cost excessive beyond a couple of hundred miles.

You can make the blocks yourself if you have the right type of soil close at hand. The procedure is messy but simple. There are tricks to it, however, and you should arm yourself with full information before attempting it. Write to the American Bitumuls and Asphalt Company, 200 Bush Street, San Francisco. They will send you literature telling you how to recognize good adobe soil and how to make the stabilized bricks.

George de Gennaro, Photo

Tile brings a touch of elegant informality to the outdoor room. Terrace pattern formed by laying two sizes of tiles

TILE . . . traditionally western

Tile is an old-time Western surfacing that has been in favor since it was introduced by the Spaniards 200 years ago. The padres laid handcrafted tiles in the patios and corredores of the missions and the Dons who followed them made good use of the material in their comfortable haciendas.

Tile has much to recommend it for garden paving. Its warm earthy browns and reds blend naturally with garden colors; its hard-fired pigments are permanent and non-fading. Smoother and harder than common bricks, tiles are easier to clean and wax, and are particularly suited to areas that are subject to soiling, such as the barbecue terrace, the potting shed, or the walkway around a swimming pool. Tiles provide a "dressy" surface that is just as suitable indoors as out; in fact, they are often installed on patio floors that extend into the house or lanai. Available in various shapes and sizes, tile can also be used for paths, stairs, countertops, or even for covering existing wooden floors.

Tile has some limitations, of course. Principal objection is its high cost of installation. Due to the high quality materials and precision workmanship that go into its manufacture, tile is much more costly than common brick. Patio title costs about twice as much per square foot, quarry tile may run two to three times more. Another cost-increasing factor is the type of foundation required for permanence. The large patio tiles may be bedded on sand or even dirt, but for real satisfaction most tiles require a solid bedding of mortar or concrete.

However, the relatively high cost need not discourage the homeowner from using tile in his garden, for he doesn't need to lay an ocean of it, and he can make artful use of small panels of tile to dress up a breezeway, a barbecue area, or a walk. It blends happily with other paving materials—providing a change in pattern and texture when used with brick, a smart contrast in color when paired with concrete or blacktop.

Some home handymen are wary of setting tile themselves, feeling that they would rather trust a professional with their heavy investment in materials. However, laying tile is well within the capabilities of the average week-end mason—providing he is willing to work with precision and care. Tile setting does require more exact workmanship than most other paving materials: the grade has to be leveled to a gnat's whisker, the tiles have to be kept scrupulously clean of mortar, and the joints struck smooth and even. The hard-fired tiles cannot be cut so easily as brick. They have to be sawed with a mason's diamond saw or else patiently whittled down with a hammer and chisel.

KINDS AND SIZES

There are several sizes, colors, and shapes to choose from, depending on the catalogue that you chance to pick up.

Outdoor floor tile is rough-surfaced in contrast to the glazed varieties used in kitchens and bathrooms. Patio tile comes in brick red; quarry tile is obtainable in tones running from gray to brick color.

Most outdoor tile is either ¾ or ⅞ inch in thickness. Tiles are obtainable in squares—12x12, 9x9, 6x6, 4x4, etc.—and rectangles—12x6, 9x6, 8x4, etc. The large, foot-square tiles are commonly known as "patio" tile. They also come in the half-size, 6x12. Other tiles are known as "quarry" tile. The patio tile is not made to such close tolerances as quarry tile, and consequently is cheaper. It can even be obtained in rough, handcrafted shapes that look like the primitive tile put down by the early settlers. Tiles are also obtainable with rounded edges for stair treads and corrugated or abrasive surfaces for high-traction needs.

Hollow tiles, such as those used in wall construction, are sometimes put down for patio flooring. Though cheaper and softer than patio or quarry tile, they are not so durable. They fracture easily when objects are dropped on them.

LAYING OUT

To save yourself the bother of cutting or chipping the iron-like tiles, you had better plan out your surfacing requirements so you can stay within the dimensions of the tile that you intend to use. Allow for ¾-inch mortar joints for the large tiles, ½-inch for the small sizes.

If you must cut tile, you will find it easiest to mark the tiles where they should be cut, take them to a stoneyard, and have them sawed with the diamond saw. If you have only a few to be cut, you can chip them to size with a narrow cold chisel. Draw your cutting line with a pencil, place the tile on a sack of sand, and, starting at the edge, nibble your way in to the line. If your patio or walk calls for a curving

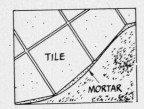
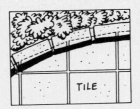

edge, cut the tiles in a series of angles that correspond roughly with the curve. You can also lay a curved border of brick on top of the rim to give the appearance of a curved edge.

Sheltered barbecue-dining terrace paved with tile set in mortar on concrete slab. Tiles arranged in running bond

Gene Hainlin, Photo

Straightforward pattern of white mortar joints makes small terrace seem spacious. Fallen leaves are easily swept off tile

Eckbo, Royston & Williams, Design; Childress & Halberstadt, Photo

Tile artfully used in combination with bricks and gravel. Tile bedded in mortar, bricks in sand. Redwood header boards

Maynard Parker, Photo

Tiles laid without mortar joints give a friendly, informal feeling to entryway, and match rustic siding, door, hardware

Clarence Cullimore, Design

Tile pattern harmonizes with adobe ranch-style home and helps to keep expansive porch in scale with house and grounds

TILES-IN-SAND

Patio tiles are sometimes effectively laid on dirt or sand. You may want to try this method if your soil is very flat and stable, if you desire an informal appearing surface, or if you need a quick, temporary floor. If it doesn't work out, you can always take up the tiles and reset them on a bed of mortar or cement.

They should be set on a shallow bed of sand so they will not have a chance to shift around or rear up when a corner is stepped on. You can place them

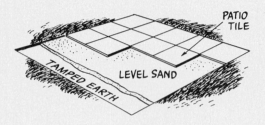

¾ or ½ inch apart and fill in the joints with sand or moss, or you can butt them tightly against each other. The latter practice will probably give more satisfaction, for the snugly fitted tiles will tend to keep each other in line. However, check over your tiles beforehand and sort them into groups of identical dimensions, for there is sure to be enough variation in their dimensions to make precise fitting impossible if you don't take this precaution. Small quarry tile or mixtures of small and large are not likely to prove satisfactory on a sand bed.

Level off the soil 1 to 1½ inches below the desired grade. Fill in hollows, cut down humps, and tamp or roll the ground until it is firm and smooth. Soak any fill until it has settled.

Place headers along the outer edge of the area to be covered with their top surfaces flush with the desired grade, allowing for a drainage slope of ⅛ inch per foot. Notch the ends of a long straight board the thickness of the tile you are going to lay and rest the notched ends on the headers. Or nail "ears" on the straight-edge for the same purpose. The lower edge will then be at the right height for the top surface of the sand bed.

Pour in sand and level it by moving the notched straight-edge along the headers. One cubic foot of sand will cover about 40 square feet ¼ inch deep, 20 square feet ½ inch deep, 10 square feet 1 inch.

Set the tile in place, starting from a corner. Give each one a tap with a block to bed it in the sand. Use the straight-edge to check evenness of the tiles as you lay them.

To keep the sand from leaking out of the bed or the tiles from creeping away from each other, leave the header boards around the edge, or set a rim of tiles vertically into the ground, or mix cement into the sand along the outside foot of the sand bed (proportion: 1 to 5).

SETTING IN MORTAR

For a permanent surface set your tiles in a bed of sand mortar.

Prepare the grade in the same manner as outlined above, but allow for a 1-inch mortar bed. You will need to order 1 sack of Portland cement and 4 cubic feet of sand for 35 square feet of patio surface. This is for 12x12 tile set ¾ inch apart. For smaller tile, you will need more mortar for the joints and should increase these figures proportionately.

Mix 5 parts of clean sand with 1 part of cement on a mixing board or in a wheelbarrow. Mix the dry materials until no streaks of gray or brown are showing. Add water and continue mixing until a smooth but slightly stiff mortar is obtained.

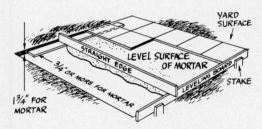

Pour the mix onto the ground, and skim it level with the notched straight-edge, as described above, and sprinkle a light coating of cement on the surface.

As tile should be laid while the mortar is still plastic, be careful not to spread a larger bed of mortar than you can cover with tile within an hour, otherwise the mortar will be set before you can get all your tile laid.

Soak the tiles in clean, clear water for at least 15 minutes beforehand. Stand tiles on edge to drain off surface water, then bed the damp tile on the wet mortar. Tap the tile in place with a hammer until it is firmly bedded. Use the straight-edge or a level to help get a smooth surface and to position the tiles into a straight line. Do not stand or step on the tiles. Stand on a plank mounted on blocks that keep it above the surface of the tiles.

Leave about ¾-inch space between each tile to be filled in within 24 hours with jointing mortar.

For jointing mortar, mix 1 part cement with 3 parts sand and add enough water to get a soft mix that will almost flow. Pour it into the joints from an old watering pot or coffee can with its lip bent to form a pouring spout. Fireclay or lime putty are not

George de Gennaro, Photo

Sweeping walk of hard-fired quarry tile, laid in running bond with white joints, leads hospitably to front doorway

John Bomberger, Design; Phil Palmer, Photo

This terrace of foot-square patio tile, laid directly on the ground, is easy to change when you want a new pattern

Maynard L. Parker, Photo

Use of tile in patios is old as the West. Here the traditional tile is laid in terrace and corredor of Spanish home

Thomas Church, Design and Photo

Tile can be effectively used in the garden in small amounts, as illustrated by this path running beside a reflecting pool

Cliff May, Design; Julius Shulman, Photo

Rough-textured double bricks laid in tile pattern and fitted around trees. Unlike tile, double bricks are easy to cut

needed in this mortar but their presence will do no harm.

Avoid pouring the mortar on the tile surface, and immediately clean up any that does spill over with damp, clean rag.

Fill the joints flush and trowel them smooth with a mason's trowel.

It is not necessary to keep the tiled surface wet after it has been laid, but it should not be walked on for at least 3 days.

LAYING TILE OVER CONCRETE

It is a simple matter to lay tile over a concrete slab.

On rough-finished concrete, clean and dampen the surface, spread a ¾-inch mortar bed and set the tile in place as described above.

Prepare smooth concrete floor surfaces by roughening with dilute muriatic acid wash or with a wire brush (see the chapter on concrete), clean, rinse well, and allow to dry; then brush with a paste of cement and water and apply the mortar as above.

To make tile non-absorbent and to brighten its natural rich color, after the tile has dried out, give the finished job one or two light coats of a colorless sealer. This will make the surface easy to clean. Do not use self-polishing wax on exterior floors.

SETTING TILE ON WOODEN FLOORING

To cover a sun-deck, stairs, or porch with tile, first make certain that the structure will support the added weight without sagging. Most floors can take the added load without harm, but it may be necessary to install additional footings to prevent sag or to keep the weighted corner of the house from settling. Patio tile on a 1-inch mortar bed weighs about 20 pounds per square foot.

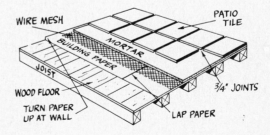

First, nail a layer of waterproof building paper over the flooring. Then stretch a reinforcing mesh of ¾-inch stucco or chicken wire and nail in place ¼ inch above the wood.

Apply a 1-inch mortar bed of 1 to 5 cement mortar (1 part cement, 5 of sand). Dust cement over the surface and bed the wet tiles in place as above.

Flagstones set in wide mortar joints give texture and pattern to this great terrace and keep it from seeming bleak

FLAGSTONES . . . outlast the house itself

Flagstones—or "turfstones" if you want to know where the word comes from—are the aristocrats of the paving materials. Unless the homeowner happens to own a quarry, he is likely to pay more per square foot for a flagstone walk or patio than for any other material he could have chosen—as much as five to ten times the cost of concrete or owner-laid bricks.

Many people feel that flagstones are well worth the investment. A flagstone pavement is as solid and durable as it looks; indeed, if properly constructed it can last forever. The subdued colors of the stone slabs—buff, yellow, brownish red, gray—bring mellow warmth to the patio; their irregular shapes and sculptured surface add pattern and texture to the garden floor.

On the other hand, some people are wary of using flags, even when they can afford to do so. They consider them cold and lifeless, feel that they add a quarry-like atmosphere to the patio. They have also seen the unfortunate effects achieved when a patchwork of colors is put down indiscriminately or when irregular-shaped stones are placed together in a dizzying pattern.

As a compromise, imitation flagstone paving can be cast in concrete with pleasing results. The color, pattern, and texture can be controlled to produce the exact effect that the designer wishes to achieve.

MATERIALS

You can choose among several different types of stone at your building material dealers. Most popular western varieties are Arizona sandstone, California slate, Yosemite granite, Utah gray, and Crab Orchard. The slabs are available in either irregular or rectangular shapes. The latter often cost more because of the cost of cutting them. Thickness ranges from ½ inch to 2 inches. In some sections of the country, flags can be obtained as thick as 6 inches. For paving over a sand bed, a 2-inch thickness is essential; thinner stones are set over a concrete slab. The ½-inch stones, normally used for wall veneer,

can be placed over concrete, but a 1-inch thickness is safer to use, less likely to fracture when you are laying it. Some types of flagstone are easily cut on the job, either with a brick set or by breaking them over the edge of a 2x4.

Dining terrace paved with flags set in wide mortar joints to match rusticity of forest furniture, rough-hewn shelter

Flagstone surfacing looks at home in patio of Spanish-style home. Flags set in mortar, give fairly even surface

FLAGS IN SOIL

Simplest way to lay flagstone paving is to put the flag down directly on the soil. If your soil is stable and well-drained, this type of paving may be thoroughly satisfactory for limited areas such as a walk. The flags will shift and settle in wet or frosty weather, but they can still be walked on.

Dig out the soil to a depth slightly less than the thickness of the flags and fit the stones in place. Chief problem is adjusting the soil so it will fit the contours of the rock.

Fill the joints with turf, or pack in good soil and plant grass seed or set clumps of creeper.

FLAGS IN SAND

For more stability, flagstones are put down on sand in the same manner as brick or adobe block. The technique described for these materials elsewhere in this book can generally be applied to setting flagstones, with a few differences.

After a 2-inch sand bed has been put down and carefully screeded, set the flags in place so they are firmly bedded over their entire surface. Make sure that there is contact throughout so the stone has no chance to develop a list.

If you are laying irregularly-shaped stones, you would be wise to put them all down so you can study the general effect before you fill in the joints. If the pattern seems too busy or exploded, you can shift stones around until you achieve the desired effect.

Fill in the joints with good soil that will support grass or a creeper. The soil should be placed so it is not flush with the surface of the stones. Shovel it into the joints and wet it down thoroughly with the hose. If necessary, add another layer in a week. Then sow seeds or plant seedlings.

If subsoil is likely to be saturated during winter months, put down an 8 to 12-inch base of gravel, crushed rock, or cinders; roll it; and set stones as above.

FLAGS ON CONCRETE

For a permanent surface, set the stones on a 3-inch slab of concrete, put down in the manner described in the chapter on concrete paving.

The flags should be bedded in mortar, spread over the concrete when it is about 24 hours old. (For instructions on mixing mortar, see chapter on building brick walls.)

If you don't mind the extra labor, you will be well repaid to try out your pattern as described above before setting the stones permanently in place. Once they are fixed in mortar, it will be too late to adjust them to correct unsatisfactory patterns. As you are going to have to live with the pattern for a long time, you had better make sure that it is pleasing.

Trowel a 1:3 mortar on the slab in small areas, just enough to accommodate one or two flags. Place the flags *dry* on the mortar bed while it is still quite plastic. Tamp in place with the trowel handle and level with a straightedge.

Thomas Church, Photo

Example of popular and attractive way to set flagstones is to fill in joints with soil and plant with creeping thyme

Rectangular flagstones cut and broken on the job to give the appearance of carefully-fitted stonework. Sand joints

Do not walk on the freshly laid flags for at least 24 hours. A plank supported on cleats above their surface will get you across newly laid patches. Fill in the joints with grout and smooth the surface with a small pointing trowel. Immediately wipe off any grout that spills on the stones with a clean, damp cloth. Clean up any excess mortar stains as described in the chapter on building stone walls.

CAST CONCRETE STEPPING STONES

Individual concrete flags to be used for stepping stones can be cast in a simple wooden form or they may be poured in a dirt mold right where they are going to be laid.

Casting in Forms: A simple, sturdy form will provide you with an endless supply of cast flags. Make it of 2x4's. Nail two corners, hinge the third, and put a hook on the fourth. Place form over building

paper, oil form, and pour in concrete mixed to 1:2:3. When concrete sets, remove form, clean, re-oil and refill. Keep cast blocks damp for 3 days.

Casting in Dirt Mold: Simplest method for making stepping stones is to pour them right where you want them. Dig out the desired contour for each stepping stone to a depth of 4 inches. Space out the excavations so the stones will be no more than 18 inches apart for comfortable walking. Toss in some spare rocks for economy, and fill in with a 1:2:3 mixture of concrete. Trowel surface smooth with a wood float. If set in a lawn, the surface of the stones should be below the lawn so the mower can pass over them. Keep damp for 3 days.

Mellowed Flagstones: For a variation of the method outlined above, you can cast the stones so they have textured surface as mellow as brick or stone.

The flagstones are built upside down in the ground mold. The uneven contour of the ground, imparted

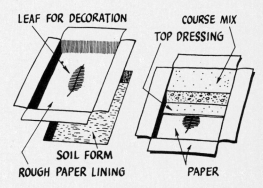

to the surface of the stones when *reversed* for use, gives them a natural appearance. No two are alike.

Philip Fein, Photo

Meandering path of stepping-stones invites the flower-lover to take his time when he passes through this pleasant garden

Floyd Cowan, Design

Chamomile creeps between irregular Sonoma stones, adding varied texture and color effects to the regular flag pattern

Floyd Cowan, Design

Flagstones are made informal and picturesque by the use of tiny colorful rock plants growing from between cracks

Philip Fein, Photo

Flagstones set into the lawn offer an hospitable approach to the Spanish gate. Turf is easily controlled around flags

Moreover, by using a paper lining in the mold, a smooth sheen can be given to the finished block, quite unlike ordinary cement and closely resembling water-worn rock surfaces.

Dig out the soil and line the bottom and sides with several thicknesses of heavy paper, such as cement sacks, or heavy wrapping paper such as is used in butcher shops.

Ordinarily, in making cement walks or steps, the standard 1:2:3 mixture is used with a final thin top dressing of cement and sand to give a smooth, hard surface, showing no aggregate or gravel. Here the layers are necessarily inverted. A thin layer (approximately ½ inch) of cement and fine plaster sand in a 1-to-2 proportion is poured first, followed, as soon as it has set slightly, by about 3 inches more of the regular 1:2:3 mix. Tamp firmly and keep moist for several days before prying up and stripping off the paper.

CAST CONCRETE FLAGSTONES

To cover a large area with cast concrete flags, you will need facilities for mass-producing the artificial stones. Casting 500 flags one-by-one can postpone the patio's completion indefinitely. Easiest way to cast the flags en masse is to build a wooden grid form that will make several stones at one filling.

The grid can be built to an angular pattern or to one that is strictly rectangular. The former requires a mitre box for precise fitting of the angles, but it can produce an interesting paving pattern. The rectangular grid is easier to fit together, and it may be built to yield square tile-shaped blocks.

The wooden form should be built of 2x4's with divisions corresponding to the finished sizes of the finished product. The inner surfaces should be smooth and slightly tapered with a plane toward the bottom to facilitate removal as soon as the concrete sets.

A good size combination of random sizes for use in walks is: one each 12x18 inches and 12x12 inches, and two each 6x18 inches and 6x12 inches. For patio

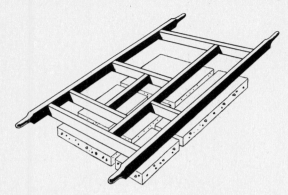

paving, larger sizes would be in better scale.

The grid is put down on the graded and compacted soil and the compartments filled with concrete. After the slabs have set, the framework is disengaged from the blocks and set up again for the next section of the walk or patio.

In using forms, you will have less difficulty removing the concrete if the forms are thoroughly saturated with water before using. Greasing or oiling the inside of the forms with old crankcase oil or soap will also prevent the cement from adhering to the wood. The use of oil or grease also keeps the forms from warping after use.

Curved Flags: For curved shapes, use a set of individual forms made of galvanized iron. Secure a dozen strips 3 inches wide, bend them to shape, and secure the ends with a cotter pin. Fill the molds, and after the concrete has set, unfasten them and set them up in the next area.

Scott-Imlay, Design; Philip Fein, Photo

Path made of large slabs of concrete cast in place. Spaces between slabs filled with stone for texture, color change

John Robinson, Photo

Terrace flooring made of lightweight concrete castings, fitted into geometric pattern. Close joints are sand-filled

Jacques Hahn, Design; Jerry Anson, Photo

Smooth terrace of cast concrete flagstones laid in subdued pattern that harmonizes with lines of French doors, shakes

Curved entrance path of concrete flagstones cast in place. Pattern repeated twice in length of walk. Joints are turfed

Litton & Whitney, Design;
Ernest Braun, Photo

Pavement of broomed concrete
laid within a redwood gridwork
unifies indoor and outdoor elements in inviting leisure room

CONCRETE . . . choose from a dozen colors, textures

Concrete once was used chiefly for narrow walks between different sections of a large garden. Now it is put to work in large livable areas where frequently the bold design of the paving reflects the color and texture of garden plant materials.

The advantages of paving with concrete are in its permanence, wearability, and low cost. It can be put in place swiftly, permitting the complete installation of patio, service yard, and walks in a matter of hours. Depending on its surface finish, it is easy to clean and polish. Its smooth surface provides a good floor for games or dancing.

The disadvantages of concrete paving are its harshness of surface, glare, and commercial feeling. Many consider it too cold and impersonal to be used as a surface in the garden. As a material, it is difficult to work with—frequently requiring special equipment and always fast work. Only when handled properly do its advantages apply. Otherwise it buckles and cracks making strength and permanence empty qualities.

Concrete requires special treatment to give it pattern or it remains a mass of artificial rock with surface glare that seems out of tune in a garden. To eliminate glare and soften the surface, gardeners

Douglas Baylis, Design and Photo

Exposed aggregate surface, made by scrubbing off smooth
top layer of concrete, adds interest and texture to this yard

have tried staining, coloring, tamping in pebbles, roughing, or exposing the aggregates.

CAN YOU LAY IT YOURSELF?

Once the homeowner has decided on a concrete patio, service yard, or walkway, he comes to the question of whether to do the work himself or have it done by a paving contractor.

Laying concrete is hard work. But if you don't take on too big a job in too little time, it can be a lot of fun. If your paved area can be broken up into relatively small areas, you should be able to handle it satisfactorily.

However, if you are in a hurry for your paving, want to be certain that it is properly installed, or if you have a sea of concrete to be laid, you are probably better off in the hands of a reliable contractor. Professionally-laid concrete will cost twice as much as the amateur-laid variety, but there are ways of shaving down this cost differential. You can save by doing the grading yourself and setting all header boards in place. You can also eliminate frills, such as colored topping, hard-troweling, or exposed aggregates. However, such temporary economies may not prove out in the long run.

If you decide to have the work done by a contractor, you would be wise to protect yourself and him by setting up written specifications for the job. You can obtain suggested specifications by writing to the nearest office of the Portland Cement Association.

CONCRETE FORMULA

Concrete is a mixture of cement, sand, gravel, and water that is bonded together by a chemical reaction between the water and the cement. The character of the concrete is determined by the proportions used for these four ingredients. The most critical relationship in the formula is the water-cement ratio; quantities of sand and gravel may be varied slightly without affecting the strength of the mass, but the proportion of water to cement must be exactly observed.

The formula recommended for garden paving is:

    1 part cement.
2¼ parts sand.
    3 parts gravel or crushed stone.

To this is added water in the amount of 5 gallons to each sack of cement. Water should be clean and pure—good enough to drink. Sand used in concrete must be clean river sand; the seashore variety won't bond. Gravel should range in size from ¼ to 1½ inches.

MIXING CONCRETE

You have several types of mix to choose from: you may buy the cement, sand, and gravel and blend them yourself by hand or by machine; you may get the sand and gravel already mixed, requiring only the addition of cement; or you may buy all three ingredients premixed, delivered to your doorstep ready to pour in place.

Philip Fein, Photo

Grid pattern of bricks breaks up monotony of large area of concrete paving. Flint in topping provides interesting texture

Thomas Church, Design and Photo

Rough pebble surface gives rich texture to concrete panels framed in brick. Stones pressed into topping while still damp

Philip Fein, Photos

1. **Redwood grids will give both a pouring form and a paving pattern when left in place after concrete hardens. Depth: 4 in.**

2. **To make a curved headboard, make a number of saw cuts halfway through 2x4 and bend board in direction of the cuts**

Hand-Mixing: You can produce first-class concrete by mixing it yourself on a platform by hand. It is slow, hard work, though, and best suited to small jobs or piecemeal laying of a large area.

You will need a pail marked off to show gallons and quarts; two shovels, one for mixing dry materials, the other for blending wet; and a large flat surface to use as a mixing platform.

Build a makeshift platform of old lumber 6 or 7 feet square. Don't use lumber that is badly warped or full of knots, as it will let water trickle through and weaken the concrete. An old square of plywood makes an excellent mixing surface; some backyard masons mix right on their driveways.

Heap the mixings on the board, one shovelful at a time, keeping the proportions in line with the formula, and blend the ingredients together. For each shovel of cement, figure about 3 quarts of water (based on an average of 6 to 7 shovelfuls of cement per sack).

To save effort, learn to use the shovel with a rolling motion, turning the ingredients under with the blade. You will find this less tiring than the scoop-lift-dump method. After you have thoroughly blended the dry aggregate and cement, scoop out a hollow in the center of the heap, and fill it partly full of water. Mix in the water by working your way around the edge of the puddle with the shovel, rolling the dry mix into the water with the blade. Be careful not to break the dam, for if much water escapes, the batch will be weakened.

If you are working with the separate ingredients, first make a trial batch to test the workability of the formula. The mounds of sand and gravel that you bought are certain to contain enough moisture to require you to vary the formula slightly. To make the test batch, spread 2¼ shovelfuls of sand on the

mixing board and add 1 shovelful of cement. Blend together until no gray or brown streaks remain. Then spread 3 shovelfuls of gravel over the cement-sand mixture, and blend until the gravel is evenly distributed. Scoop out the center, pour in 3 quarts of water, and mix it in. If the trial batch is too soupy, add a small amount of sand or gravel. If it is too stiff, cut down the quantity of sand or gravel in the next batch and proceed with the job, mixing henceforth to the adjusted formula worked out in this batch.

Machine-Mixing: Old timers will tell you that there is a limit to the amount of concrete that you can comfortably mix at one time on a board. They recommend that you rent or borrow a portable mixer and a large wheelbarrow. Most efficient mixer for a one- or two-man job is the half-bag machine. These are revolved by gasoline or electric motors or by hand. If you have the choice, stay away from the latter—they're not much fun, although turning the crank is easier than shovel-mixing.

Toss into the revolving drum 1 cubic foot of sand and ½ sack of cement. Allow them to mix until the blend is free from streaks of brown or gray. Add 1½ cubic feet of gravel and continue mixing until the pebbles are uniformly coated. Then, empty 2½ gallons of water and allow the wet mixture to tumble

3. Curves give an interesting change of pace, relieve geometric appearance of paving squares. Set between firm stakes

4. Wet, plastic concrete is smoothed out with wood "float." Variety of finishes can then be applied from rough to slick

for 2 or 3 minutes. Finally, pour into a wheelbarrow and dump into the forms. This load should cover about 8 square feet of 3-inch paving, 6 square feet of 4-inch, 4 of 6-inch.

Ready-Mixed Concrete: If you have a vast amount of concrete to pour, you can pass along the labor of mixing to the concrete dealer by ordering "ready-mix" or "transit-mix" delivered to your backyard.

Ready-mix is prepared in a giant truck with a revolving drum that mixes it while the truck is on its way to your home. Surprisingly, concrete in this form usually costs about the same as the home-made variety. There is a "catch," though. Transit-mix companies will not usually deliver less than a cubic yard (enough for about 100 square feet of 3-inch paving) and they charge penalty rates if the truck is not emptied within a short time. There is also a limit to the distance that the companies will carry the wet concrete (usually 1½ to 2 hours' drive from plant).

There are further considerations to be weighed before inviting the truck into your garden. For one thing, the truck carries more concrete than one person can lay. It can spend a half hour in your yard and remorselessly empty enough plastic concrete to keep you and several willing neighbors hopping for the rest of the day. If your patio is inaccessible from the street—uphill or down too steep a slope—you must forget the idea. If your lot is laid out so the truck can back its stern close to your patio, you had better find out if your driveway can support the heavy load. Planking the driveway with 2x12's should prevent its cracking under the weight. Planks can also be used to form a roadway across a lawn—but a dry lawn, by all means.

ESTIMATING AMOUNT REQUIRED

Garden paving should be 3 to 4 inches thick. If sections of it are to double as a driveway, plan for 6-inch thickness.

To determine how much material to order, compute the square footage to be covered with concrete, and refer to this table which shows the amounts needed to fill 100 square feet:

Separate Ingredients	Thickness of concrete		
	3″	4″	6″
Cement (sacks)	6	8	12
Sand (cubic feet)	13	18	26
Gravel (cubic feet)	18	24	36
Ready-mix (cubic yards)..	1.0	1.3	2.0

Note that concrete mix, either wet or dry, is sold by cubic measure. The dry ingredients occupy about ⅔ of their volume when mixed with water and must therefore be ordered in excess of the volume of the area to be filled. Wet mix, on the other hand, can be ordered in quantity that equals the anticipated volume of the slab.

In some localities, concrete ingredients are sold by weight rather than by cubic measure. A cubic foot of sand or gravel weighs between 90 and 120 pounds, depending on how damp it is. A sack of cement equals a cubic foot and weighs about 100 pounds. A ton of sand contains about 22 cubic feet; a ton of gravel about 20 cubic feet.

For small jobs, you can also buy dry-mixed cement sand-gravel put up in 100-pound sacks under various trade names. As each sack will only yield about 4 square feet of 4-inch paving, this is an uneconomical type to use for general paving. It is very handy, however, for patching or for piecemeal work. Try to get fresh stock that has not lain in a warehouse for several months or been exposed to dampness.

GRADING AND FORMS

If you are planning to pour a large area, you will find it easier to do if you block it off in smaller squares that you can fill one at a time. Some week-

Henry Van Siegman, Design; John Robinson, Phot

Simple patio of broomed concrete in redwood framework. Posts for screen are supported on piers incorporated in paving

end masons have found that a 5-foot square of 4-inch concrete is just about par for a Saturday afternoon for a man working alone. With help, of course, the area can be increased, but you will still find it convenient to put it down chunk by chunk.

Best way to block off the area is to set either permanent or temporary header boards in place. For permanent headers, use redwood, cedar, or some other rot-resistant wood; for temporary forms, any straight-grained wood will do. Use 2x4's for straight lines, double 1x4's or tripled ½x4's for curves. Green wood or wet wood will bend more easily than dry.

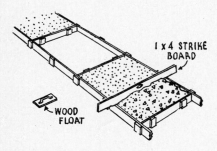

Coat temporary forms with crankcase drainings or whitewash so they can be removed without sticking to the concrete. If you are going to remove the forms, pour sections alternately. After these have hardened, enough to hold their shape, remove the form cross strips and pour the intervening slabs.

The permanent headers may be locked into the concrete by driving spikes part way into them so they will protrude into the concrete. However, it may be necessary someday to remove the headers —they do wear down, splinter, and discolor—so you may prefer to leave them loose. Concrete will shrink away from them when it sets.

Brace all forms and headers firmly with stakes driven deep into the ground. Plastic concrete has a way of bursting its way out of fragile forms.

Set headers so their top surface is flush with the grade you plan for the concrete. Check levelness with a spirit level set on top of a long straight board rested on opposite headers. Adjust height of headers to permit slope away from the house. Plan for a drop of ⅛-inch per foot.

Level the soil with your shovel and remove weeds, sod, trash. If you have to dig out the soil, overfill the cavities with dirt and tamp solidly in place. To settle the soil, wet it two or three times ahead of pouring day. Night before, wet area thoroughly so the soil will be damp when you pour onto it. Dry soil will suck moisture out of the concrete and weaken it.

POURING

Best time to pour is early morning before the sun gets too hot. Avoid pouring on hot dry days or in freezing weather. Excessive heat will make the concrete set too quickly, before you have a chance to dress it properly, and it will interfere with curing. In cold weather, you can warm the sand and aggregates by running a length of stovepipe through the pile and keeping oily rags burning in it or by warm-

John S. Bolles, Design; Esther Born, Photo

Wide-spreading terrace is kept in scale by checkerboard of 4-foot squares of exposed aggregate paving and redwood planks

ing the water to not over 175°, but don't heat the mixture above 80°. Do not lay it in freezing weather; never pour on frozen ground. Concrete that has been frozen while fresh will never be very strong. If you are overtaken by an unexpected freeze, cover the slab with an insulating layer of straw, canvas.

Pour each batch of concrete into the forms and tamp into place within 30 minutes. The back of a flat shovel makes a handy crude trowel for smoothing it into place. Dump successive loads so the plastic concrete runs into the batch previously laid, not away from it or on top of it.

It is best to pour in all-over layers. For a two-day job, roughen the top surface of the first day's pour just before it hardens. Next day, sluice it off with a hose, and with an old broom, brush on a creamy paste of cement and water just before adding the fresh batch.

When concrete fills to the surface skim it level with the edge of a long, straight board. Check the surface with the level and smooth irregularities with a flat wooden trowel known as a "float." (You can buy one at a hardware store or make it yourself from a piece of hardwood 1x11x4½ inches plus a substantial grasp handle.)

As a rule, reinforcing steel is not needed for patio paving in mild climates. But if the concrete is laid over very unstable soil, is likely to be subjected to a wide range of temperature variations, or is scheduled eventually to carry a structural load, such as the wall of an additional room, reinforcement should be added. The Portland Cement Association recommends ¼-inch bars, spaced on 6-inch centers, (or an equivalent wire mesh) laid on top of a base course 4 inches thick and followed immediately by 2-inch finish course. On unstable earth, a slab may need reinforcement in the lower part. A competent engineer should be consulted for advice on reinforcing problems.

SURFACE FINISHING

For the final finish, you can choose from a variety of surface textures ranging from a hard, slick finish to a rough pebbly surface. Choice of the surface to suit your needs will depend upon the over-all plan of your garden, relation of paved areas to the house, the ways in which you and your children will use the paved area, the amount of time you will want to give to maintenance.

1. *Hard Finish:* A hard glossy finish is one of the easiest surfaces to take care of—and one of the toughest to put down properly.

It is easily swept, mopped, or waxed, and it makes an ideal dance floor. On the other hand, such a surface seems too slick and machine-like for garden paving, it reflects the sun to an uncomfortable degree, and its slickness may be a hazard to children and old people. It is usually used indoors in preference to outdoors; so if you plan eventually to incorporate your patio into the house, you may want to anticipate the move by putting down the slick surface to begin with.

How It's Done: The slick finish is obtained by passing a steel trowel over the surface after it is partially hardened. It takes plenty of muscle to

Redwood gridwork left imbedded in service area, removed for dichondra planting in terrace. Plant box of concrete block

Concrete paving blocks were poured in place; after construction forms were removed, grass was planted between blocks

smooth the reluctant concrete, and some masons avoid this labor by troweling while the concrete is still wet. For a really durable finish, however, the troweling should not be attempted sooner than 30 to 45 minutes after the concrete has received its rough finishing, after the sheen or shiny film of surface water has disappeared. If it is done while the slab is still plastic, the troweling will suck fine particles of sand and cement to the surface, weakening the slab and yielding a sandy surface that will flake off in time. For proper finish, the first troweling should be done lightly, just to smooth over the float marks. The second should be applied with enough pressure to make the trowel ring when it is drawn along the surface. Deluxe jobs call for four trowelings.

2. Wood-float Finish: The wood-float finish provides a surface that is smooth but not slick. It is soft enough in appearance to be unobtrusive in a garden setting—providing it is not spread to the far horizons.

It is produced with the mason's wooden trowel (float) that is used for rough finishing. The resulting surface is smooth enough for easy cleaning, for dancing, and for easy movement of furniture.

Objections: It reflects sunlight glare and it soaks up food stains because of its porosity.

How It's Done: When the concrete has been screeded level, smooth off the surface with a wooden float. Bring the surface up to grade with the trowel, fill in valleys, and reduce the hills. Be careful not to overdo the troweling while the concrete is still plastic, as this will bring too much water and fine material to the surface. Allow the concrete to harden somewhat, then go over it again with the trowel for your finish surface.

3. Broom Finish: If you want a slightly roughened surface, you can secure an interesting texture by brushing the green concrete with a push broom. Use a straw or steel broom to produce a heavy ribbed finish like combed plywood; use a hair broom for a light corduroy grain.

Either texture is rough enough to cut down surface glare and provide good traction. The rough broomed surface is often used for steps and ramps where surefootedness is essential, although the ribbed texture wears smooth under steady traffic. Both surfaces are dust catchers: dirt collects in the grooves whenever the slab is swept and it has to be flushed out with water for adequate cleansing. The rough-ribbed texture is too slow for dancing, but the fine-brushed surface may be made passable by dressing it with floor wax (2 coats paste, 1 of liquid) or powdered soap or boric acid.

How It's Done: Brooming should not be attempted until the concrete has set hard enough to retain the marks of the bristles. For the rough finish, brush the concrete after it has been floated; for fine brushing, sweep the surface after it has been troweled smooth. Use a board to stand on so your weight will not mar the surface. You'll need a pair of boards—one to stand on and one to retreat to when you have finished an area.

4. Exposed Aggregate Finish: In recent years, the once-popular exposed aggregate finish has come back into favor.

It is one type of paving that looks at home in a garden. Its pebbly surface blends with the uneven modeling of the plantings, the textures of lawn and cultivated soil. Architecturally, it pairs well with natural wood siding, grapestake fencing, and other

James A. Lawrence, Photo

Grid pattern gives interest to wide driveway. Strips of grass in the joints connect lawns on both sides. Hard finished

Douglas Baylis, Photo

Pairing of concrete with bricks gives sidewalk interest, and contrast in texture, pattern. Aggregates exposed in concrete

softwood garden structures. It can also provide contrast in texture to the severe planes of a modern home. Its uneven texture takes the curse out of a large expanse of paving, especially if framed within wooden grids. It doesn't glare and it provides sure traction in any weather.

In its disfavor: it collects dirt and dust that can only be cleaned out by forceful washing with the hose or a scrub brush; and stains on the pavement around the barbecue, under the table, or in the children's play corner, defy erasure. In its rougher forms, its abrasive surface is tough on the knees of crawlers or on small fry who fall on it; and the gravelly texture makes a miserable dance floor, gives furniture the wobbles.

How It's Done: This finish results from scrubbing or brushing the surface to expose the form, textures, and colors of natural rock in the concrete. If you can get them, select colorful aggregates that will take a polish, such as crushed black slag or feldspar, gray granite screenings, marble chips. After the slab is down, start the brushing while the concrete is still

quite "green," preferably within 24 hours. At this time the surface film of concrete can be removed by scrubbing with a stiff wire brush and water.

Don't wait until the concrete hardens or the brush will not remove the surface mortar. Continue scrubbing until aggregate is uniformly exposed. If the

surface is too hard for water to affect it, use a scrubbing solution of 1 part muriatic acid in 4 to 5 parts water. Rinse with clean water after scrubbing.

CLEAN-UP

When the job is finished, clean out the mixer and rinse off the tools to prevent their rusting.

CURING

Wet down the finished concrete and cover the surface with clean sand, canvas, or straw to retard evaporation. The surface should be protected from the sun and wind for at least 10 days and kept damp for 7 days. During cold weather, the slab should be kept covered but it does not need to be watered.

During very hot, dry weather, you can give sure protection by ponding, that is, by building a dirt or sand dam around the rim of the slab and covering the entire surface with an inch of water.

COLORING

Concrete is an ornery, unpredictable material to color. The durability and intensity of its coloring are likely to be affected by many factors. The relative proportions of the ingredients in the slab, the degree of enthusiasm with which the finish coat was troweled, the chemical composition of the pigments used, the age and porosity of the concrete, the amount of iron in the water—these and other complications can make the task of coloring concrete a tricky operation at best.

Concrete may be colored either when it is fresh or after it has hardened. With proper materials and

Floyd Cowan, Design

Concrete paving permits introduction into garden of freely designed decorations such as this trapezoid-shaped lily pool

Philip Fein, Photo

Dust-on pigment is sprinkled on the surface of the fresh concrete and worked in with float for permanent coloration

careful following of directions, the color may be successfully applied at either stage.

COLORING WET CONCRETE

When concrete is in its wet, raw state. it can be successfully colored by adding powdered pigment to the plastic mass. One method of doing the job is to lay a colored concrete topping on a natural concrete sub-base. The second method is simpler: the color is dusted on the surface of the fresh concrete. It is then worked into the surface with a wood float.

Pigments: The pigments used for coloring concrete come in the form of finely ground powder. They are obtainable from building material dealers in about eight basic colors — black, yellow, buff, brown, red, dark red, blue, and green—and they can be mixed together to produce two to three hundred different shades.

All the colors are metallic oxides—some natural, some manufactured, but paint chemists advise that pigments made with iron oxide are likely to stand up best. Depth of color depends upon the amount of pigment used. Light shades are achieved by going easy on the powder; for delicate pastels, use white cement and sand.

Cost of the pigments varies widely according to brand and according to color. Usually, dark red is the cheapest and blue and green the most expensive.

Blending Pigments with Cement: Whether the pigments are dusted on new concrete or applied in a topping layer, they are usually mixed first in dry form with cement and aggregates (sand or fine rock). You have to be downright finicky about this, or you won't get uniform color. If you do the mixing yourself, first measure out quantities and do it accurately, particularly where work requires several batches. Even a slight variation in amounts of pigment and water is likely to cause considerable dif-

ference in the final color.

Mix the cement and color pigment through a screen with ⅛-inch mesh. Pass the materials through the screen as many times as necessary and until the mix looks uniform in color. The reason for all this fussiness is that the pigment doesn't dye the cement; it merely forms a coating around the cement particles. You have to mix it until each particle is coated with color. *It's a good idea to lay sample panels and give them time to cure under the same conditions you'll have on the job.* Wipe them with a rag dipped in equal parts of paraffin oil and benzine to bring out the color.

1. *The Dust-on Color:* The dust-on method does not give so deep color as the pigmented topping, but it is easier to do and it will give satisfactory color in ordinary use around the garden.

There are various ways of applying the color. Veteran professionals scatter the raw pigment on the concrete just as it comes from the box—a feat that would result in sure disaster if an amateur were to attempt it.

Or the pigment can be carefully mixed dry with gray or white cement in a ratio of 5 to 10 pounds of pigment to a sack of cement. The colored cement is then scattered over the damp concrete, about 1 sack to 100 square feet. This is a method that the amateur can master, but he would be wise to practice on a small panel or two.

Third method is to mix pigment, cement, and a light aggregate such as sand together before applying. Proportions recommended by the Portland Cement Association are:

1 part cement.

1 to 1½ parts dry, screened sand.

8–15 pounds of pigment per sack of cement.

The amount of pigment to add will vary according

Douglas Baylis, Design and Photo

Patio with exposed aggregate; dichondra set into grid and curve pattern. The barbecue firepit extends to soil underneath

Eckbo, Royston & Williams, Design; Ron Partridge, Photo

Hillside terrace paved with smooth-finished concrete in redwood grid. Planting inset designed to solve drainage problem

to the brand and the color intensity desired. A one-sack batch should cover 200 to 300 square feet.

In the fourth method, part of the work is done for you at the factory, where pigment, cement, and aggregates are machine mixed and bagged in 100-pound sacks. With this type of mix, your only task is to sift the contents of the bag onto the concrete and trowel in the color. Because of the highly concentrated pigments used in these mixes, a little goes a long way, and most manufacturers recommend application of only 40 to 50 pounds to 100 square feet of concrete. Cost of this type is slightly higher than the other methods above.

After the concrete base has been leveled and surface water removed, spread the dust-on color mixture evenly over the surface of the slab.

Work the mix into the surface of the slab with a wood float. Discontinue floating when the surface becomes wet. Then stop for a while and when the water sheen produced by floating has practically disappeared, give the surface a light going over with a steel trowel. The fewer strokes required to smooth the surface, the better.

2. *Colored Topping:* Standard proportions for topping mix are 1 part cement, 1½ parts sand, and 1½ parts clean pea gravel or crushed stone. Cement and color pigments (5 to 10 pounds per sack) are combined before the concrete is mixed. Use not more than 5 gallons of water per sack of cement. You want topping as stiff as possible but still workable.

For garden paving, walks, or driveways, you can lay the colored topping over the concrete base course before it hardens. This way you get a good bond.

The topping layer should be about ½ inch thick. As soon as it is placed, level it with a strikeboard and smooth the surface with a wood float.

COLORING HARDENED CONCRETE

Once the concrete has hardened, it can be colored by applying a pigmented wax or special paint to the surface or by etching the color into it with an acid stain.

Each method has its advantages and disadvantages. Under favorable circumstances, satisfactory color can be obtained from any of the three dressings—wax, paint, or stain. Under unfavorable conditions, these three finishes can also turn out to be quite disappointing.

1. Waxes

Of the three methods, wax is the easiest to apply, but it must be renewed periodically and some types become slippery when wet.

There are some paste waxes on the market that have been specially developed for application on concrete. The waxes contain pigments that color the concrete if it is porous enough to absorb the wax. For some varieties, it is necessary to open the pores of the concrete with a bath of dilute muriatic acid (see discussion below under PAINTS).

To apply paste waxes, first clean the surface of oil (see below). Then rub on the paste with a cloth or brush it on. Let it stand long enough to harden. This usually takes only 15 minutes, but on dense, old concrete, the time needed may run to several hours. After the wax has hardened, rub it down with a hand or mechanical lamb's-wool buffer.

Areas that are subjected to foot traffic will require rewaxing every 6 to 12 months, depending on the volume of traffic. Some waxes used for coloring may also be used to dress stained concrete.

Douglas Baylis, Design; Julius Shulman, Photo

Generous squares of exposed aggregate keep wide-ranging terrace in scale. Sunken firepit in center for social fire

Mason Weymouth, Photo

Rough-textured exposed aggregate pavement breaks up sun's rays and prevents glare. Paving contained within wood grids

2. Stains

Stains will withstand heavy traffic and strong sunlight. They are relatively inexpensive and are not troublesome to apply, although they require a succession of applications that consume three or four days for the entire process. Stains cannot be used successfully on a rough surface—such as exposed aggregate—and they have a relatively limited color range.

Staining is accomplished by a chemical reaction of the concrete with the stain, some of which contain a muriatic acid base.

Best results are obtained from stains if the concrete is relatively new or unleached by moisture and if the surface is fairly smooth. The concrete should be cured at least six weeks, however, to avoid a mottled color. On uncured spots of the surface, for example, the greens will be very dark. No matter what you do or how carefully you apply stain, colors may still vary somewhat because of differences in density of the concrete. For maximum penetration of stains, waterproofing and curing compounds should not be used in the concrete.

Preparing the Concrete Surfaces: Clean the surface thoroughly before staining. Remove wax and grease with a solution of 1 pound of tri-sodium phosphate, obtainable at any paint store, dissolved in 1 gallon of warm water. Scrub with a stiff fiber brush and flush with clear water. To remove old paint: mix 1 can of lye with a gallon of water. Go at this *slowly* so that the lye solution won't foam up and spatter on your skin or clothes. Pour the solution over the concrete. After soaking the surface with this solution for 1 hour, scrub thoroughly and flush with clean water. Let dry. The paint should now come off easily. Repeat if necessary. *Caution: wear rubber gloves, galoshes or rubber shoes, and protect your eyes with glasses while mixing, applying, or cleaning with lye solutions. Both lye and trisodium phosphate are extremely alkaline substances. Avoid rinsing them off into planting beds containing acid-loving plants, such as azaleas, rhododendrons, etc. A sand dam along the edge of the slab can be used to prevent the solution from washing into a bed.*

Staining the Surface: Apply stain according to the manufacturer's directions. Most stains are applied in two preliminary coats, 8 hours apart, and one wax-finish seal coat. *Caution: Keep stain from coming in contact with plantings. The acid in the solution will damage vegetation on contact. If spilled on the soil, however, it has only a temporary effect.*

Stain coverage varies with porosity of the concrete, but usually one gallon provides two coats for about 200 square feet.

Finish coat should cover approximately 800 to 1000 square feet to the gallon.

3. Special Concrete Paints

Crux of the paint problem is this: All concrete contains alkali. Concrete absorbs moisture like a sponge if the slab is not waterproofed when it is laid. Moisture seeping through, particularly where the concrete is laid next to the ground, carries alkali to the exposed surface. The alkali solution reacts with the conventional oil paints in such a way as to form soap. This saponification results in softening and

Thomas Church, Design; John Robinson, Photo

Foot-wide mowing strip around edge of lawn provides secondary pathway, eliminates need for hand-clipping lawn edges

Douglas Baylis, Design; Julius Shulman, Photo

Rough texture of exposed aggregate paving provides needed interest in expansive terrace, harmonizes with the plantings

non-drying, and the paint cracks, peels or wears off quickly.

Special concrete paints and enamels have been developed to help lick the alkali-moisture problem. Depending upon care in application, traffic and moisture conditions, such surfaces will retain original fresh-

ness more than one year and then may be renewed. They are considered tricky to repaint, however, because the solvent dissolves the old paint when the new is applied.

These special concrete enamels have a rubber base which resists alkali and moisture. They come in a range of colors and can be applied directly to fresh concrete. They dry quickly and give reasonable traffic wear.

Preparing the Surface: The method of applying rubber-base enamels depends upon whether bare or formerly painted concrete is to be covered. In both cases, concrete must be prepared for the enamel, by etching the surface.

You can begin this while the surface is still damp. For etching, get commercial grade 32 per cent muriatic acid from hardware or paint store. Mix 1 part of the acid with 2 parts of tap water to get the proper 10 per cent concentration. One gallon of diluted acid should etch approximately 300 to 500 square feet. *Caution: Mix in enamelware, wooden bucket, or stone crock, but not in metal. Wear rubber gloves, galoshes or rubber shoes, and protect your eyes with glasses while mixing and applying.*

Pour the diluted acid over the surface and brush it vigorously with a long-handled brush. After the acid ceases to bubble, go over any remaining smooth spots with full-strength acid until all sheen disappears. The concrete should have a uniform, open-faced granular texture similar to that of fine sandpaper. When all bubbling ceases wash off with a full stream of tap water. Let the floor dry thoroughly.

Note: Be careful flushing off the muriatic acid solution to keep it from reaching the surface roots of plants or from spilling on grass. It will burn grass and may injure root systems temporarily. One way to prevent rinse water from spilling into garden beds is to line edge of concrete surface with a sand dam, and mop up the solution or channel it into unplanted areas. Effect of the acid on the soil is quickly overcome by the soil's buffer system which neutralizes the acidity.

Preparing Prepainted Surfaces: Where ordinary oil paints have been used, you must first remove them before rubber-base paints can be brushed on, as the latter contain strong solvents that will lift the old coatings.

Loose and scaling paint should be scraped and wire-brushed. To make the job easier, dissolve 6 heaping tablespoonfuls of cornstarch in 3 quarts of warm water. Then dissolve 1 can of lye in a gallon of cold tap water, being careful not to spatter skin or clothes with the lye. Then pour the lye mixture into the cornstarch solution. Stir to prevent lumpiness. Swab on with an old brush. After it dries you should be able to scrape off the paint easily with a knife, wire brush, or steel wool. Repeat if necessary.

The floor must next be etched, following etching instructions already given. After etching, as soon as the floor is dry, you are ready to begin painting. Use two coats of concrete enamel. Thin the first coat 10 per cent with special thinner to make it stick better.

How to Apply: Paint is usually brushed on in two to three coats, depending on anticipated traffic. Follow manufacturer's instructions carefully.

Esther Bruton Gilman, Design; Max Greene, Photo

Stiff brush used for final clean-up on pebble mosaic before front doorway. Design areas are separated by metal strips

PEBBLE MOSAIC . . . rich accent for the garden

Most gardens have one or two spots where a tastefully placed panel of pebble mosaic can serve to relieve the bleakness of a stretch of paving, give accent to a garden sanctuary, or spell welcome at the gate or threshold.

This ancient art is within the reach of almost any degree of talent. When you make a pebble mosaic, the whole family can get into the project. The smallest members can gather rocks. Family council can work out design and colors—maybe an animated map of your locality, an Indian design or even a doodle brought home from kindergarten.

The cost of pebble mosaic is negligible, and if your experiment in pebble paving fails to satisfy you, you can chop it out with a mattock and start over (or fill in with standard paving). You can practice on small samples—a square under a downspout, a bird bath—before launching your major work of art.

PATTERNS

In general, keep your designs very simple. Make strong outlines and mass your colors boldly. You will probably find it helpful to make a preliminary sketch on wrapping paper large enough to cover the

Leslie Kiler, Design

Rich-looking panel of pebble mosaic relies on bold and simple elements in its design. Brick frame tones it down

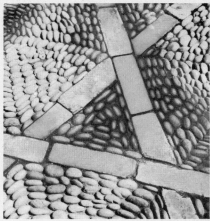

Leslie Kiler, Design

Slim rounded pebbles from seashore and streambeds make best materials, set on edge in mud or mortar. Simple designs best

entire area. If your design is very large, it can be sketched out in sections. Lay your pebbles over the paper to find out how many you'll need. If you feel hesitant about embedding your final design, check it with an artist.

Keep your pebble mosaic in scale with the outdoors. Borders are best about 1 to 2 feet wide, while squares in the garden walk can be at least 3 by 4 feet in dimension.

You can find many ideas for designs in books on old Spanish architecture.

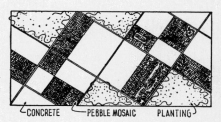

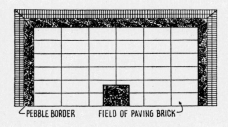

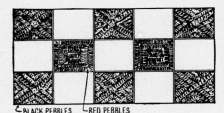

As suggested in the paving diagrams, pebble mosaics should be confined by fixed materials. From both the mechanical and artistic standpoint, they work out best when used as insets in surfaces of brick or concrete. Fixed borders keep the mosaic tightly in place.

SETTING PEBBLES IN MUD

There are two ways of setting the pebbles: they may either be set in mortar or they can be embedded in clay mud.

Setting in mud is the procedure that has been used for centuries in Spain. Some mosaicists prefer this traditional setting to cement mortar because they feel the color of the background harmonizes better with the pebbles than cement mortar. If the clay is properly prepared, it will form almost as permanent a base as the mortar.

First provide drainage with from 2 to 6 inches of gravel topped by 1 inch of sand. If natural drainage is poor, use full 6 inches of gravel.

Plan your design so that you can continue the mosaics over a period of time. Making them insets in a field of paving will allow you to do one section at a time.

Sort the pebbles for texture and color and grade them for size. Pebbles that are smooth, hard, and beach-washed are best.

Leslie Kiler, Design

Although pebble mosaic often seems best in small panels, it can be used for large areas, as this setting demonstrates

Florence Alston Swift, Design; Douglas Baylis, Photo

Abstract design of pebble mosaic splash pool shows fresh departure from traditional pattern. Pebbles set in concrete

Screen dry clay soil until it is fine as dust. With the dust, fill in the area where the pebbles are to be inserted to within pebble depth of the surface of paving.

Wet the clay a small section at a time until it is the consistency of dough. Set pebbles on end and close together in the mud. First set them a little high and then press with a plank to embed them evenly and firmly. Sweep off the excess clay.

By breaking up the clay soil and then puddling it, you drive out all the air so that when dry it is almost impervious to water.

SETTING PEBBLES IN MORTAR

For true permanence, you may prefer to set the pebbles in mortar on a concrete slab. This may be advisable if the panel will be in the path of heavy traffic, as at the front door or gate, or if it is likely to be subjected to erosion due to garden sprinkling or rain runoff.

Mix your mortar with 1 part cement, 2 parts sand, and enough water to give you a mix that doesn't run but spreads easily. You can spread a ½-inch layer of this on top of the concrete slab all at once and level it off with the sides of the board frame in which the slab was poured. But be sure you can get all your rocks placed in the 1- to 2-hour period you'll have before the mortar sets. If not, put the mortar in by sections, using a stiffer mix. Smear in a square foot of mortar, fill in the design with rocks, then cut back the dry edges of mortar and smear in another section.

Your rocks must be wet to give a good bind. You'll have to work more or less freehand since there's no easy way to trace a design on wet mortar.

When the design has been in place 2 to 3 hours, the mortar will have set unless weather is unusually moist. Then tamp dry sawdust down between the

rocks with a piece of 2x4. The sawdust pushes the stones into the mortar, pushes the mortar down around each stone so it stands out, and levels off the whole thing. After an hour or two, brush off the sawdust with a broom. Try a tentative pass with the broom to be sure stones are firm so you don't budge them. In another hour or so, wash the sawdust off with a brisk fine spray from the garden nozzle.

If you want to be extra careful, you can cover your design with 2 or 3 inches of sand or sawdust, and keep the covering damp for a week. Then remove smears or smudges of mortar with a stiff brush and a mixture of 1 part commercial muriatic acid to 2 parts water. (Don't make this mixture in a metal container. And be sure to wear galoshes, rubber gloves, and goggles to be absolutely safe.)

Florence Yoch, Design; Aplin-Dudley, Photo

Seahorse panel before doorway is made of flat rocks set edgewise in mortar to withstand traffic in and out of door

Pleasant garden terrace paved with redwood rounds bedded on sand. Space between the discs is filled with quarter-rounds

BLOCKS AND ROUNDS . . . texture of the forest floor

Perhaps no surfacing looks more natural in a garden setting than wood paving. Its warm color and soft texture seem to bring something of the forest carpet into your garden.

There are several popular ways of putting it in place. Round discs, cut straight through the trunk of a redwood, cedar, or cypress tree, can be put down on sand in random fashion like flagstones. Square blocks, usually sliced off discarded railroad ties, can be set like bricks in standard paving patterns. Or, for a more formal effect, strips of lumber can be placed in duckboard fashion.

Let no one convince you that wooden paving is permanent surfacing. If you would like to use it, plan for its eventual renewal or replacement. Under ideal circumstances, it will last a good many years; but under unfavorable conditions, it may have to be torn out in two or three.

The reason for the impermanence of this type of paving is easily understood. The blocks or rounds are usually set in place so the end grain is in constant contact with ground moisture that seeps up through the sand bed. The open grain soaks up the water like a sponge. This produces an ideal environ-

Thomas Church, Design

Blocks used to pave gardener's terrace adjoining house and cold frame. Area rimmed by seat wall used for plant display

ment for bacterial and insect growth and the wood either rots away or succumbs to insect invasion. This is a severe test of the decay resistant qualities of any wood; and even the varieties known for their durability, such as redwood, cedar, or cypress, disintegrate in time. Blocks cut from railroad ties often last the longest, because the ties were at one time pressure-treated with creosote.

A thorough application of a toxic wood preservative should lengthen the lifespan of wooden paving by several years. You can choose among several effective solutions. Five percent solution of pentachlorophenol will give good protection, but since it

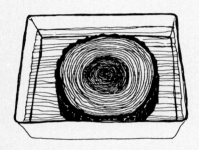

is toxic to plant life, it may discourage any plantings that you might want to grow between the blocks or rounds. Copper naphthenate is another excellent preservative, but it imparts a green tint to the wood.

Be sure to ask for a variety of preservative that has a toxic agent included in the formula to discourage insect invasion. Many preservatives simply shield the wood from water penetration and do not protect it from insects with a hankering for it. Termites will take up housekeeping in rounds or blocks —even those cut from redwood, which is traditionally hostile to them.

Blocks and rounds have a further limitation. They are sensitive to weather. Best in shady spots, they crack and warp in sunny locations; they will also freeze and split in heavy frosts.

END-GRAIN BLOCKS

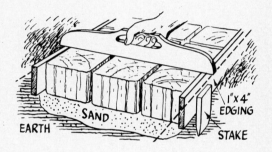

To set blocks in place, first excavate area of walkway or patio to a depth of 1 inch greater than the thickness of the blocks. Set a 1x4-inch redwood header around the edge of the area to be covered, half of it below grade.

Steps formed of redwood rounds ranging from 6 to 36 inches in diameter. These require preservative treatment for long life

Philip Fein, Photo

Pavement formed of squares cut from redwood beams, laid on sand in brick pattern. Sand poured and tamped into joints

Tamp the ground and cover with 1 inch of sand. Place blocks level with the edging, separated from each other about 1 inch. Adjust their spacing until they fill in the area to be covered, then pour or sweep sand into the space between them. Tamp the sand down into the joints with a narrow piece of wood.

An alternate method of laying the blocks consists of pouring a well mixed clay mud (not adobe) on the tamped earth. The blocks are then "puddled" into position, allowing the mud to work up into the spaces between blocks. Level the blocks by placing a strong board across them and pounding with a heavy tool. This type of surfacing is most useful on elevated ground where drainage is not a problem.

Blocks may also be set in cement mortar (1:3) like bricks. (See chapter on brick paving.)

For best results, use long blocks, say 4x4x8, so they won't float on soggy soil.

ROUNDS

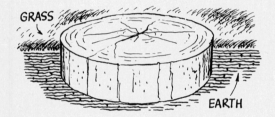

Rounds are easily set in place. Grade the soil as described above, but omit the header boards. The large discs are less likely to slip around than the smaller blocks and do not need a restraining edge.

Thomas Church, Design; Philip Fein, Photo

Garden path paved with redwood squares. Color and texture blend with the forest-like setting, dry-stone retaining wall

Philip Fein, Photo

Rectangular redwood blocks used as stepping stones through lawn area. Blocks cut from rough 8x8 timbers, and treated

Thomas Church, Design; Philip Fein, Photo

Block paving used effectively in more formal garden design. Note ease with which blocks can be cut to follow curved edge

Put down a 2-inch sand bed, place the rounds on top of it in random style, and fill in between them with soil that will support moss or grass instead of sand. Gravel, crushed brick, or pebbles may also be used effectively.

PARQUETED

The terrace shown is designed particularly for areas where drainage might become a problem. Redwood 2x4's are laid upon the tamped earth at 28-inch

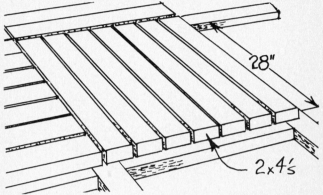

intervals in both directions. Upon this base short lengths of 2x4's are placed as shown, and secured in that position by galvanized nails. Rough lumber is used for the foundation; finished lumber for the flooring. Flooring pieces are laid with a space of 3/8 of an inch between them.

If the surface of such a terrace is placed below the level of the surrounding garden, drainage tiles should be laid at its edges, in a gravel-filled ditch about 6 inches below the surface of the ground.

Garrett Eckbo, Design; Julius Shulman, Photo

Steps of barkless redwood rounds lead from concrete terrace to the grass terrace below. Rounds bedded on concrete base

Jerry Anson, Photo

Large rounds cover entire terrace and surround swimming pool. Interstices filled solid with broken rounds. Cool, dry

Lytton & Whitney, Design; Philip Fein, Photo

Wood squares set end-grain. Pebbles pressed into quarry dust in open joints break up monotony of the block pattern

Osmundson-Staley, Design; Philip Fein, Photo

STEPS

Osmundson & Staley, Design; Theodore Osmundson, Jr., Photo

Use broad treads. These steps, made of redwood, set on stringers, have 16-inch treads, lead from house to play area

Douglas Baylis, Design; Ernest Braun, Photo

Break a steep slope with landings. This street-to-entry stairway has three landings. Steps are of redwood and bricks

Osmundson & Staley, Design; Theodore Osmundson, Jr., Photo

Make entrance steps wide. Concrete steps with birds eye gravel pressed into surface to give nice texture and safety

Thomas Church, Design; Ron Partridge, Photo

Choose friendly, tough materials. Field stones, laid in mortar, framed with ivy and ivy geranium, are appropriate to scene

STEPS . . . how to plan and build

Amateur step builders usually approach their step construction projects with the idea that a garden step should cover the shortest distance between two levels. If the slope between levels is steep, the steps will just have to be steep, too, and there's nothing to do about it.

Actually, a direct level-to-level approach is seldom either necessary or wise. And steps from house to garden or terrace to terrace should never be approached without considering the tread and riser relationship.

When comfort, design, and safety are considerations the relationship between tread and riser is not a hit and miss affair. Actually, there's a preferred relationship for every situation. If the steps are designed for a leisurely approach, you'll use one combination. If your steps lead to a service area, you'll use a different one.

If you want steps ideally suited to children and oldsters, you will cut down on the height of the risers. Outdoor steps should be in scale with the outdoors—more generous than indoor steps. Let's work with a few tread and riser combinations which may help you solve your step problems. Landscape architects and engineers say that these are the best combinations:

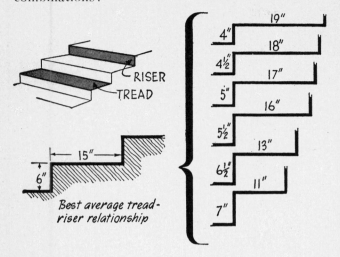

It's possible, too, if you want a ramplike stairway, to use as much as a 28-inch tread with a 4-inch riser or to use a 2 or 3-inch riser with treads over 20 inches. No tread on a garden stairway should be less than 11 inches—and you should not use one that narrow unless absolutely necessary.

For a step that's a good in-between average, one that will work well for both adults and children, one that's a happy medium between ramp and ladder, use a 6-inch riser and a 15-inch tread.

The materials you use may have some influence on tread and riser combinations and certainly the slope may influence your choice.

How do you apply these riser-tread combinations to your own particular slope? First, figure out the change in level.

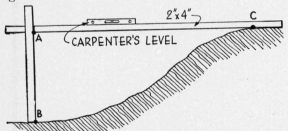

You can find it by setting up a measuring device like that shown above. The distance from A to B is the change in level, the measurement from A to C is the minimum distance your steps should travel.

You'll rarely find a slope where the change in level and the distance to be covered are exactly right for one of the tread and riser combinations that we listed above. But the slope is not immutable; usually you can shape it to fit the steps you want. In the sketch above, if you simply built steps to fit the slope, you would end up with a bad tread and riser relationship. But you could use the *average* garden step with the

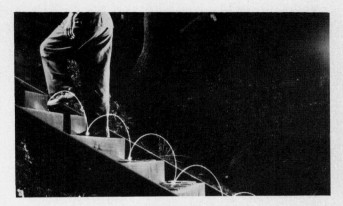

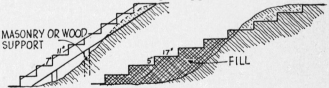

Ernest Braun, Photo

You can't talk yourself out of expending energy when you go from level to level. But the closer steps come to normal walking stride, the safer they are, and the easier for all ages

6-inch riser and 15-inch tread and simply apply it to the slope.

Or you could use a more leisurely approach on the same bank—or a steeper approach.

You will have to cut the bank or fill under your steps to make the slope fit your stairway. And the slope may influence your choice of material. If you build out from a bank, for instance, you might prefer to make wood steps and leave the space open underneath.

Sometimes you must work out your steps within two fixed points—if the house and a garden path restrict the space you can work in, for instance. Then your choice of riser and tread will be limited to a combination that fits in the space that's available. But that doesn't mean you must use a bad tread-riser combination just because it fits. You don't have to go straight up. You can use one of the prescribed combinations, then fit it to the slope by breaking the distance with landings. Or you can curve the steps or zig-zag them.

It's a good idea, anyway, to break a long, steep slope. A steep, straight-up-the-hill stairway gives you a sense of exhaustion even before you start up.

The best way to work out a step problem is to plot it on paper, much as we have done in the sketches above. Make little diagrams drawn to scale. In some cases, you may prefer to rough out your steps on a 1 by 12-inch board. Mark your steps on the board, then see how they fit the slope. Step width is mostly a matter of proportion, of choosing a width that best fits the garden. But there are some minimum requirements. You should figure 4 feet the minimum for a one-person stairway, 5 feet for a two-person stairway. Of course, access or auxiliary steps built for purely functional reasons, can be as narrow as 2 feet.

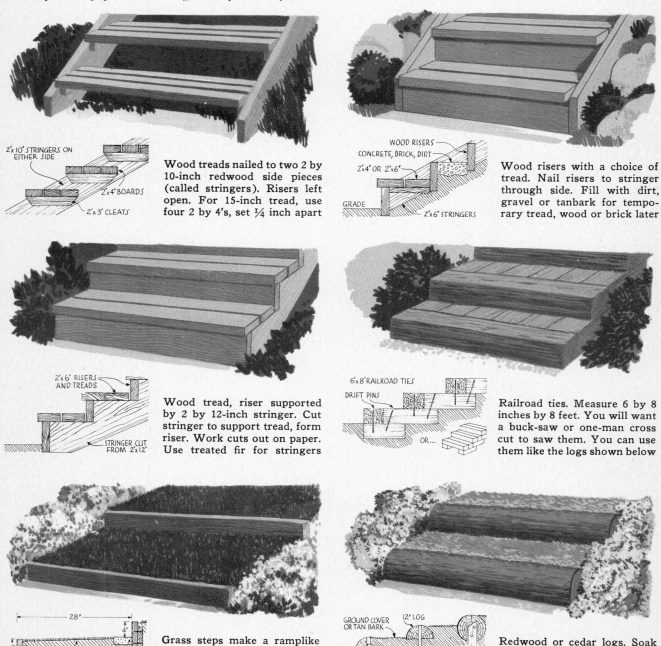

Wood treads nailed to two 2 by 10-inch redwood side pieces (called stringers). Risers left open. For 15-inch tread, use four 2 by 4's, set 1/4 inch apart

Wood risers with a choice of tread. Nail risers to stringer through side. Fill with dirt, gravel or tanbark for temporary tread, wood or brick later

Wood tread, riser supported by 2 by 12-inch stringer. Cut stringer to support tread, form riser. Work cuts out on paper. Use treated fir for stringers

Railroad ties. Measure 6 by 8 inches by 8 feet. You will want a buck-saw or one-man cross cut to saw them. You can use them like the logs shown below

Grass steps make a ramplike change in level. Treads should be wide, broad for mowing, while risers can be anything. For mowing strip, use brick

Redwood or cedar logs. Soak in pentachlorophenol, copper, or creosote solution. Suggested for ground cover: dichondra, arenaria or mother-of-thyme

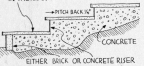

BRICK RISERS
BRICK TREADS
MORTAR

Brick treads, risers, set in mortar. Design variations almost unlimited. If there's much fill underneath them, use reenforced concrete to give support

BRICK IN MORTAR
2"x8" WOOD RISER
PLUMBER'S TAPE
STAKES OR PIPE

Brick treads, wood risers. Best support is pipes. Use 3-foot length, place one about every three feet. Tamp soil solidly before laying in the bricks

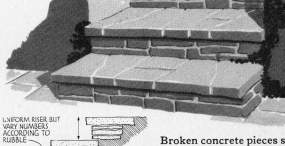

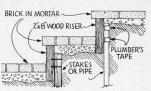

12" QUARRY TILE IN MORTAR
PITCH BACK ¼"
CONCRETE
EITHER BRICK OR CONCRETE RISER

Brick-red quarry tile treads, with brick or concrete risers. For wet-weather safety, pitch tile to back. For a rougher tread, use tile rough side up

UNIFORM RISER BUT VARY NUMBERS ACCORDING TO RUBBLE
1" OVERHANG
LAID UP DRY OR IN MORTAR

Broken concrete pieces stacked on top of one another make tread and riser. You can shape pieces to fit by using hammer. If dry laid, plant in the cracks

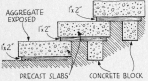

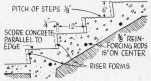

AGGREGATE EXPOSED
1"x 2"
1"x 2"
1"x2"
PRECAST SLABS
CONCRETE BLOCK

Make pre-cast slabs any size. Ones sketched are 4 by 20 by 48 inches. Overlapping 3 inches gives 17-inch tread; the 1 by 2 provides a 5-inch riser height

PITCH OF STEPS ⅛"
6"
4"
12"
SCORE CONCRETE PARALLEL TO EDGE
⅜" REINFORCING RODS 18" ON CENTER
RISER FORMS

Concrete steps need reenforcing steel, careful forming. For safety, score edge near nose of step, expose pebbles, or sprinkle surface with pea gravel

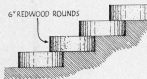

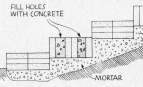

6" REDWOOD ROUNDS

Six-inch slices of redwood or cedar logs are suitable for a narrow access stairway. Keep slices 15 inches in diameter. Treat with wood preservative

FILL HOLES WITH CONCRETE
MORTAR

Hollow-center concrete blocks, alternately flat and on end so every other riser has holes exposed. For those on end, fill holes in tread with concrete

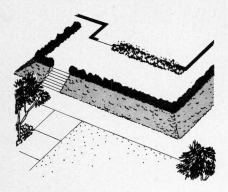

Minor steps are inexpensive. Here they preserve the privacy of upper terrace, isolate noises of the play area below

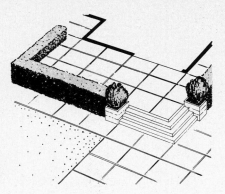

Corner steps point to living center of the garden, invite you to the shade and shelter of garden room and lower terrace

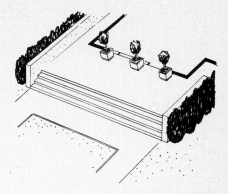

Big scale steps do double duty—as retaining wall, change level. They also bring both levels into closer relationship

Broad, directional steps give a spacious, friendly feel to entry. Or use them in back to direct traffic to center of garden

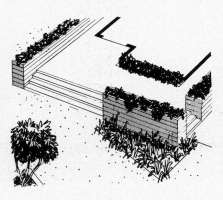

Major and minor. Broad steps lead from sidewalk to entry, narrow ones from drive. Or house to terrace, service yard

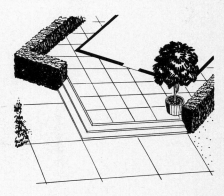

Projecting steps tie upper and lower terraces together, give sitting space when activities spread over both levels

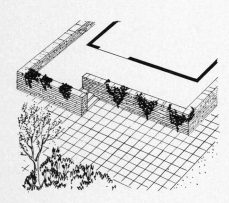

Hidden steps help walls preserve privacy of upper terrace, help make possible almost complete separation between levels

Curved steps embrace the whole level below, let you choose your own path to barbecue, flower bed, and work center

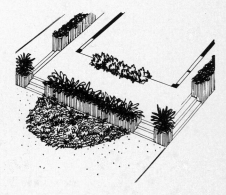

As a plant box base. Steps and boxes do retaining wall job. Placed right, helps in separation of different garden areas